MW01095044

Lives that Speak
and
Deeds that Beckon

Lives that Speak
and
Deeds that Beckon

A HISTORY OF THE UNITARIAN SOCIETY
OF WELLESLEY HILLS

John Hay Nichols

Unitarian Society of Wellesley Hills
WELLESLEY, MASSACHUSETTS

Copyright © 2016 by John Hay Nichols

All rights reserved. This book or any portion thereof may not be reproduced or used in any manner whatsoever without the express written permission of the publisher except for the use of brief quotations in a book review.

Printed in the United States of America

First Printing, 2016

Unitarian Universalist Society of Wellesley Hills
309 Washington Street
Wellesley, MA 02481

Book Layout ©2013 BookDesignTemplates.com

Lives that Speak and Deeds that Beckon/ John Hay Nichols —1st ed.
ISBN 978-1539723141

To my wonderful wife Nancy

who bore with me through research and writing and contributed

her own thoughts along the way

Rank by rank again we stand,
From the four winds gathered hither,
Loud the hallowed walls demand
Whence we come and how and whither,
From their stillness breaking clear,
Echoes wake to warn or cheer;
Higher truth and holier good
Call our mustered brotherhood.

Ours the years' memorial store,
Hero days and names we reckon,
Days of brethren gone before,
Lives that speak and deeds that beckon.
One in name, in honor one,
Guard we well the crown they won;
What they dreamed be ours to do.
Hope their hopes and seal them true.

By John Huntley Skrine, 1884

Contents

PREFACE

IN JUNE OF 2015, the minister and the president of the Unitarian Society of Wellesley Hills took me to lunch and made two propositions. First, they wanted to ask the congregation to appoint me as their minister emeritus. I had served two prior congregations as a settled minister and subsequently ten congregations as an interim minister. But my twenty-three years as religious leader of this Society is a source of considerable pride to me. I was thrilled to accept the honor.

They also wondered, since I would be entering retirement, if I would be interested in writing a history of the congregation. Since writing such a history had been a fantasy of mine for several years, I readily agreed. Every minister has frequent encounters with the history of the congregation he/she serves, but under the pressure of more immediate concerns there is never enough time to explore what other stories that history might tell. Now I had that chance.

Church records generally exist in dusty record books with deteriorating bindings, and they are stored in an obscure part of the church. Coupled with whatever is written through records and memoirs is an oral history, which lingers through the generations. Sometimes it conveys truth not found anywhere else. Sometimes it is legend. Sometimes, even if flat out wrong, it helps to illuminate the themes that have defined the congregation. I have covered these official bases—the dusty volumes in deteriorating bindings—and upon occasion supplemented them with stories and observations that—though unverifiable—ring true to me after twenty-three years as the minister of this particular church. I have also searched back issues of the *Wellesley Townsman* and the *Boston Globe* to get a view of what local editors and reporters found noteworthy.

The leaders of a congregation are a collection of individuals who have reached beyond anything for which they have ever been prepared to steer and occasionally to harness the restless energies of a liberal church. They are led by professional ministers who are meeting a new set of obstacles and challenges with every congregation they serve. As in any accomplishment that requires other people to participate, no one is ever certain they have achieved what they started out to do. This book will reflect their hopes, dreams, and doubts. I hope it will also reflect their courage going forward.

The book title *Lives that Speak and Deeds that Beckon* is taken from the first hymn we sang in Wellesley Hills every September of every church year during my ministry. It is also—or used to be—the processional hymn of the annual Service of the Living Tradition at the UUA General Assembly, a service that recognizes and honors the Unitarian Universalist religious professionals who are new, retiring, or deceased. The hymn "Rank by Rank Again We Stand" was written in the nineteenth century by John Huntley Skrine for a book of hymns to be sung by students in the British public schools. It seems more appropriate to me as a way of honoring the "lives that speak and deeds that beckon" in the long history of a liberal congregation. These are not famous people who have sustained our congregations and moved us forward, but their works do speak and their deeds call us on to accomplish a little more.

ACKNOWLEDGMENTS

I particularly want to thank reference librarians in the town of Wellesley and at Harvard University. Cyra Coady, the church administrator in Wellesley Hills, put up with my frequent raids on the church records with warmth and good humor. Artemis Joukowsky, grandson of Waitstill and Martha Sharp, gave me a great deal of help in understanding the Sharps' work in Europe. I also want to thank Marc Schectman, the UUSWH historian who brought the historical records into better condition to find and to use. Thanks as well to Mark Harris who previewed the manuscript with an eye for historical inaccuracies. My editor Bev Koteff has made this a far better book than it would have been without her considerable effort. I am grateful to Emily Koteff Moreano for designing the book's cover and providing graphic guidance and to Bill Koteff for his technical support throughout this journey. John Pattillo, then president of the congregation, and the Reverend Sara Ascher opened the door and made it possible.

SETTLED MINISTERS
UNITARIAN UNIVERSALIST SOCIETY
OF WELLESLEY HILLS
1871 - 2000

1871 – 1899	Albert Buel Vorse
1899 – 1909	John Snyder
1910 – 1917	William Henry Ramsay
1918 – 1919	Charles Frances Potter
1920 – 1933	Walter Samuel Swisher
1934 – 1935	James Luther Adams
1936 – 1944	Waitstill Hastings Sharp
1945 – 1970	William Brooks Rice
1971 – 1974	Robert Erwin Senghas
1977 – 2000	John Hay Nichols

CHAPTER 1

Who Was Jesus?

JOHN ADAMS AND Thomas Jefferson were Unitarians. The same can be said of several other men with whom they drafted and signed the Declaration of Independence. This Unitarian faith in the ability and duty of men and women to govern themselves and even to determine their own religious beliefs is central to the intellectual revolution that is at the heart of this country's birth.

Still, the origins and convictions of Unitarianism are not well known even in a town like Wellesley where the Unitarian Society is one of its older religious institutions. It all started with Jesus.

Unitarianism has its roots in an ancient dispute over who Jesus was. Most people assume that the gospels answer this question and provide a consistent account of his life and teachings. However, for several hundred years after Jesus' death many things were not so clear to those who attempted to follow him. The gospels give us no eyewitness accounts of his life. They were shaped by writers each of whom had a different slant on Jesus' character, his teachings, and his relationship to God.

Many believed then—and now—that Jesus Christ was God who had assumed human form to redeem humankind from its perpetual sinfulness. Holding another point of view, fourth-century Christian priest Arius taught that Jesus was somewhere between divine and human—not fully God, not fully human; therefore, the worship of Jesus as if he were God was wrong.

When the Roman emperor Constantine became a Christian, he was appalled to find that the leaders of his new faith were badly divided about the most basic teachings. So he called a conference at Nicaea to resolve matters. Perhaps he let it be known that his imperial self with all of his attendant power was leaning toward the idea of Jesus as God. Not surprisingly, the Council voted in favor of its emperor's views and wrote the Nicene Creed, which defines the faith of many Christians today.

Those who still disagreed—followers of Arius and others—were branded heretics, and what had been a legitimate difference of opinion became a fighting matter, a heresy, and punishable by death. These "heretics" were the spiritual ancestors of today's Unitarians, although the issue that became their heresy then no longer matters very much.

Time passed. During the Reformation, ideas that had been suppressed for hundreds of years got a new hearing. Among these were the teachings of Polish scholar Faustus Socinus that Jesus was fully human, a man with a special God-given mission, but not God in any way. Socinian ideas spread throughout Europe, finding particular acceptance in Holland, Poland, and Transylvania, where eventually the king became a Unitarian, "uni" meaning one God, not three. In 1568, King John Sigismund of Hungary issued the first act of religious toleration in the Western world, declaring that no one in his kingdom shall be persecuted for his or her religious faith, which is a gift from God.

As the Age of Enlightenment began to dawn in the eighteenth century, Unitarian and Socinian ideas were becoming known throughout Europe. Unitarian churches were formed in London and throughout England. Liberal religious ideas eventually came from there to America, partly through the teachings of Joseph Priestley who also formulated the concept of oxygen. Because of his support for the French Revolution and other unpopular causes, Priestley and his family members were forced to flee England for Philadelphia, where in 1794 he started one of the first Unitarian congregations in America.

The late eighteenth and early nineteenth century in America was a time of great promise for Unitarian and Universalist ideas. The thirteen colonies had just overthrown the strongest standing army in the world and become a testing ground for democratic ideas. New technologies were beginning to promise a life of greater ease, better communication, and easier travel. Scientists were now intellectually able to go where previously they had been forbidden to go. The God of earlier generations—who seemed quick to judge and slow to approve of humankind—was gradually replaced in the minds of men and women by the deist's God who had established a beautiful world of opportunities and expected men and women to make the best of them without divine help or interference.

In writing the Declaration of Independence, Thomas Jefferson penned the words that God "created all men equal." Slavery was still practiced and even encouraged in some parts of the country, but many of the Declaration's signers were Unitarians or Universalists who believed that everyone should be considered equal politically and religiously. Over the years this conviction became even more strongly felt.

The next fifty or sixty years were a time of great optimism, and Unitarian Universalist ideas have had their greatest appeal in optimistic years. Many of these ideas found a sympathetic reception in colleges and universities, particularly in those that prepared men— and in those days only men—for the ministry. This was particularly true of Harvard.

In the first half of the nineteenth century, Harvard sent men who had become Unitarians at Harvard into the ministry, particularly to the parish churches in the Greater Boston area. These young men often replaced older men who had preached a Calvinist's god and the assurance of either hell or heaven depending on how righteous a person was. Parishioners had heard about these new ideas that Harvard's new preachers were presenting, and many now found them much more congenial; however, not all were convinced.

While some parishes quietly chose one Unitarian minister after another until the congregation eventually acknowledged that they had become a Unitarian church, conservatives in other parishes fought hard to hire preachers of the old faith.

In some congregations, the conservative minorities barricaded the church to prevent the pulpit from being usurped by a liberal on Sunday morning. In at least one congregation, a conservative and a liberal preached at opposite ends of the church to their respective constituencies. In a few instances, the conservatives walked out and built their own church next door. One Unitarian church with deep roots in our nation's history placed a plaque on its front telling all who cared that this was "The Church of the Pilgrims." The breakaway congregation that built their edifice next door erected a plaque announcing that this was "The Church of the Pilgrim's True Faith."

In another community, the conservatives built their own church across the street but situated it in such a way that when the Unitarian and Trinitarian congregations left their respective meetinghouses after worship, they confronted each other. One of them solved this problem by turning its entrance ninety degrees to the right so that neither congregation would have to meetinghouses greet the other after church. When the dust cleared, the Unitarians were in charge of the old in many of the western suburbs.

Many of the new ministers coming out of Harvard to take over from the first generation of Unitarian clergy were Transcendentalists.

As Unitarian Universalist historians Andrea Greenwood and Mark Harris explain:

> Transcendentalism is part of a larger Romantic movement that engulfed Europe and America in the late eighteenth century. Rejecting the dry rationalism of the Age of Reason, Transcendentalism evoked an immediate and emotional response to life. . . . The Transcendentalists rejected John Locke's "sensationalism" and argued in favor of intuition and direct inspiration. The Transcendentalists believed that every person could experience the divine personally and immediately.

While Transcendentalism had an impact on nineteenth century Unitarianism, it is likely that around the year 1871—the time of the founding of the Unitarian Society of Wellesley Hills—that impact was less in New England and more in the Midwest. New England Unitarians considered themselves liberal Christians. That probably includes the group of forty or so who left the Congregational Society of Wellesley Hills to start attending the First Parish of Needham in order to hear Unitarian preaching there.

Gathering a Congregation

IT WAS GOING to happen. In the first half of the nineteenth century, Unitarian and Universalist ideas were common currency in American religious circles. Although Wellesley had been a quiet country town called West Needham and later Grantville, the coming of the railroad through Grantville changed everything. People who had learned liberal religious ideas from Boston-area Unitarian congregations moved out to the suburbs and wanted to attend churches where they would be most comfortable. In the area now called Wellesley Hills, there was no Unitarian or Universalist church.

Since most of these new Grantville residents were liberal Unitarian Christians, they tried the Village Church and the Hills Congregational Church hoping to find something they could support. Those who attended the Hills Congregational Church were not happy with the preaching. Louise Austin, who with her husband had been members of a prominent Unitarian church in Boston under the leadership of James Freeman Clarke, mentioned the Hills Congregational Church in her memoir about the founding of the Wellesley Hills Unitarian church:

They had a minister who felt it his duty to preach the old Calvinist doctrines, which were not always pleasant to hear. There were some radical people in town, and they tried several times to have some liberal preaching . . . but never succeeded in doing so.

At about the same time that Mr. Austin and I came there, there were 4 or 5 families who were also Unitarians. Mr. A. B. Vorse was then preaching in Needham. They sent us over that way to see if they had a minister who would be acceptable to us.

This scouting party liked Rev. Albert B. Vorse's sermons and asked him if he would be willing to travel to Wellesley for preaching in the afternoons. If you can imagine the slow progress of a horse and carriage along Great Plain Avenue in the pre-pavement era, you can appreciate that this was no small commitment on the part of Vorse. He eventually found that health issues prohibited him from keeping his commitment. The committee heard other ministers but did not like them nearly as well as Vorse, so they were very pleased when his health issues cleared up and allowed him to continue what had been a pleasant arrangement.

Yet the Wellesley Unitarians wanted their own church building, and they wanted Vorse to be their minister—not Needham's. He was not averse to leaving Needham after a short stay for Wellesley where he felt he would be better paid.

As it turned out there was a building in Wellesley that could be made into a chapel and might even look like one with some money, a lot of sweat equity, and a good deal of commitment. According to Mrs. Austin's memoir, "There was a small hall named Maugus Hall. It was owned . . . by several gentlemen of the town and used for lectures or anything that should come up, and the high school used it during the week."

Adding to the description of Maugus Hall many years later, Wellesley Hills Unitarian minister Rev. Waitstill Sharp wrote:

Maugus Hall—in some records called the Railroad House—had long
served as the social center of Grantville and the forum for various
good causes. It had been built as an equipment shed for the railroad.
Here in 1847 the thirty Orthodox people of North Needham had
met to launch their enterprise—today the Wellesley Hills
Congregational Church. Here had occurred Grantville's wildest
free-for-all fight, the McClellan Riot of 1862, a brawl between the
local Republicans—never known for their shrinking timidity—and
the Copperhead Democrats.

This struggle was so violent as to set all-time standards in these
parts for all future differences of opinion. Newspapermen
dispatched from Boston to report the Grantville riot were denied
entrance to the conflict at its height when they arrived. Nothing
daunted, they filed eyewitness reports of the action. But as there
were no windows in the Hall, at the same time, they could have
seen nothing from the lawn.

Mrs. Austin's memoir notes, "We hired the hall for Sundays and
evenings. They ran a series of lectures by James Freeman Clarke, Julia
Ward Howe, Charles Ames, F. Higginson, Mary Livermore, Susan B.
Anthony, and many prominent suffragettes."

Maugus Hall was also used by a loosely organized group of men
who sponsored regular lectures featuring abolitionists, suffragettes,
and other quite liberal speakers. A few members of this association
were also involved in the founding of the Unitarian church, but others
apparently resented the trappings of religion brought into what they
had considered a purely secular space. As it turned out, this group did
not own Maugus Hall. John Shaw, who did own it and was also a
member of the Unitarian congregation, sold the building to the
Unitarians. Interestingly, Maugus Hall stood on the site of the current
chapel.

Mrs. Austin's memoir continues:

One of our lecturers suggested that we should buy the hall. We had a recommendation from the Norfolk Conference [of Unitarian congregations] to which we belonged to aid us in securing the money. Several of the Maugus Hall shareholders threw in their shares, and we had $1,625 to raise. My sister Rebecca and I took the recommendation with us and went to see Mr. Edward Everett Hale [former chaplain to the U.S. Senate and at this time minister to the South Congregational Church of Boston]. He was at once very much interested for us. "Such a small sum to be raised and so much to be gained," he said. He gave us a list of ministers to go to and see and [we] went to Dr. Gannett [minister of the Arlington Street Church] who gave the names of two parishioners. Several people volunteered money to build a church but saying that if it proved to be a radical church they would be sorry they had given $1.00.

My good pastor, James Freeman Clarke [minister of Boston's Church of the Disciples where Louise Austin, her husband, and family attended before moving to Wellesley], gave me several letters of recommendation. After the whole amount had been raised, our own people came forward and we soon had enough to make the hall into a very pleasing little chapel. Mrs. [name illegible] made a cross to be put in place of the sign "Maugus Hall." We found there was a very radical element among us who contrary to our pledge [presumably to various donors] wanted the building to still keep its name and be used for discussion and anything that should come up.

Mrs. Austin's writings about the Maugus Hall purchase reveal the first and only hint that these early founders were not all of one mind. Given the times, there could have been two radical elements; they were either politically radical or religiously radical. The context of her remark strongly suggests they were religiously radical, which probably means they were not Christians but free thinkers, agnostics, and/or secularists—contrary to the Christian identity of the majority of the group founders. Mrs. Austin's account continues:

After our work [on Maugus Hall] was completed we expected to have it dedicated but finding that there was some opposition we thought we might not be able to continue but that Sunday Mr. Vorse in his prayers, his reading, and his selection of hymns gave a dedicating service, and we said as we went home that our little chapel had been dedicated. [Hence, Vorse conducted a building dedication service without actually calling it one.]

The radical element continued to create turmoil over a Christening service [an earlier version of what we would call a service of dedication]. They withdrew [their contributions] thinking it would crush us, but Rebecca [Eaton] never knew the meaning of the word "fail" and stimulated us to greater exertion [to raise money to replace the money that had been withheld by the "radical" element].

This conflict raises the question of what religious symbolism these founders preferred. The picture of Maugus Hall that the congregation used in its promotional materials is slightly vague as to what is on the top of its steeple. Sharper pictures make it absolutely clear that there is a cross on the top of the steeple, just as Mrs. Austin's account tells

Maugus Hall, first building of USWH

us that a wooden cross was fashioned for the inside of the sanctuary despite the protests of some. These founders were late nineteenth-century liberal Christians. They were not Trinitarians. They did not believe that Jesus died to atone for the sins of humanity. They did not celebrate the Resurrection. Many could not have told what the cross meant to them. Probably the cross represented the tradition that united them in some way that was important for them to argue over and finally affirm.

Interestingly, when former minister Waitstill Sharp wrote his short history of the Society in the 1940s, the question of the cross atop the steeple never came up. Probably some took it for a weathervane, and others simply reflected that a cross was what they assumed would be on a church steeple. However, it did come up many years later when the Society was seriously involved in planning a major campaign to build a new sanctuary and convert the old church building into classrooms for its growing religious education program. At that point the architects redrew the building without a cross on the steeple, but the final building blueprint left the cross in place.

In 1870 several individuals representing roughly forty men and women petitioned the state that they wanted to become a religious corporation. The petitioners were Charles Gavett, Elisha Livermore, John W. Shaw, George H. Howisson, Oliver C. Livermore, Oliver Smith, Charles H. Dilloway, David C. Perrin, Josiah Osgood, Isaac Sprague, S. Harris Austin, Rebecca Eaton, and Louisa E. Austin.

They affirmed in their petition that they came together under the name of "The Unitarian Society of Grantville" for the purpose of "the worship of God and general religious purposes and the holding of church property therefore." To this end they formed a Standing Committee that stood in the place of the congregation to conduct the monthly business of the Society. Two things about this newly formed Society were remarkable. The first is that women were included from the beginning in the vital decisions of the congregation. After all, they had been listening to lectures from world-renowned suffragettes for at least ten years. Rebecca Eaton was the Society's treasurer and, for all intents and purposes, their moving force.

Sharp's historical account emphasizes that Rebecca Eaton was "the irresistible" will of the congregation:

> The church owes its life and early nurture to the fires of her dominating executive talent. Moving into Grantville from membership in James Freeman Clarke's Church of the Disciples in the South End of Boston, she and her unmarried sister Miss Elizabeth lived in the household of their married sister, Mrs. Harris Austin. This house stood on Washington Street near Eaton Court. Miss Rebecca was possessed of one driving conviction: the need of Grantville for a Unitarian church. She was twenty years its treasurer, serving until April 21, 1891. Her strong solemn figure can be remembered even now [1941] tramping through the snow of a winter morning to light the furnace fire in the chapel. She was always accompanied by her great Newfoundland dog and by her nephew Mr. Isaac Sprague, who she drafted as an apprentice to learn the art of heating and sweeping out as only an Eaton would perform these arts in the temple. Miss Eaton is remembered as approaching members on almost any occasion with the words, "Do you think that you are giving all that you can afford to give?" No offering plates were offered in the early years but a box was placed in the vestibule for gifts. It was the insufficient voluntary offerings of this box that Miss Eaton went about, self-commissioned, to supplement—the Unitarian conscience of Grantville incarnate!

Membership in the Society was open to anyone without the expectation of rental fees for the pews. At that time many congregations continued the policies of the past in which members were asked to rent a pew that would be their family pew for the year. In some congregations, the more favored pews fetched a higher rental value but for the same reason came with a higher social cache. It was a little like living and worshipping in the fancier section of town. By contrast, the founders of the Society were quite proud that they were a "free" congregation open to leadership from all men and women from all economic strata.

Who were some of these incorporators? Charles Gavett was a clerk in a dry goods store. John Shaw was a real estate broker who was incredibly generous to many of the institutions in the new community. George Howison was a schoolteacher, and Oliver Smith a farmer. Charles Dilloway was an insurance claim adjuster, and Isaac Sprague was an artist who was particularly well known for his sketches done for John James Audubon. S. Harris Austin was a dealer in Japanese and Chinese art. Among the ranks of other members were clerks, schoolteachers, farmers, artists, and local idealists. At least two—the Sawyers—had once been members of Brook Farm, a utopian experiment in communal living. Collectively, this early founding congregation looked more like the typical UU congregation of the twenty-first century than the movers and shakers of the New England business world who populated the nineteenth-century Boston area Unitarian congregations.

What did they want to do together? This group wanted to worship in a congregation where they did not have to translate words that were said into their own religious language. They wanted to have fun together, and they did. They wanted to experience shared silence. They wanted to be alerted to and aroused by the issues of the day. They wanted to believe there would be comfort for them should their lives lead them through the "valley of the shadow," and they hoped they could be of comfort to someone else.

Why did the incorporators call their congregation a "society" rather than a "church"? Many still ask this today. The assumption that contemporary Unitarian Universalists bring to this question is that they wanted to make it clear they were not Christians who would have called their congregation a church. This is not true of this particular instance.

To understand the answer to this question, it is important to know that in seventeenth and early eighteenth-century New England, the church was a collection of people who believed they had had a direct experience of Christ; on the basis of that experience, they affirmed together certain specific beliefs called a covenant. As the Puritan culture waned, the number of people who could make that statement greatly diminished, and the expected covenant was relaxed so that the "fallen away children" of the original Puritans could attend church with their parents. Still, the notion of being a church was bound up with believing certain specific things. In addition, the law of the Commonwealth of Massachusetts probably defined a church as an institution that was centered on Christ.

Members of the old First Parish churches did not see fit to change the names of their congregations even though it had become clear that they contained many Unitarians, Universalists, and people of more diverse beliefs than had been true only a few years earlier. They still thought they were a church despite no longer being 100% Christian. However, congregations founded as Unitarian or Universalist and seeking incorporation in the nineteenth century called themselves societies because the state legislature would not allow them to do otherwise. Hence the religious congregations in Newburyport, Carlisle, West Newton, and the Unitarian Society of Wellesley Hills were incorporated as societies.

In April of 1885, after the name of the village in which they were situated changed from Grantville to Wellesley Hills, the Standing Committee voted to petition the legislature "to change the name of the society to the Unitarian Church of Wellesley Hills." One month later, the June 15 Standing Committee minutes report, "As the legislative committee on churches refuses to change the name from

"Society" to "Church" it was voted 7 to 2 to change the name in accordance with the views of said committee to The Unitarian Society of Wellesley Hills." Nonetheless the congregation continued to know itself and to be known by the community as the Unitarian Church of Wellesley Hills.

What was it like to be a member of this congregation? Louise Austin remembers, "The life of the church in those days was full of activity. A course of lectures together with coffee parties through the winter months, a two- to three-days fair usually held in a tent on the lawn beside the chapel, a mid-summer picnic . . . were always events in which the whole community was interested and all of which affairs augmented the church finances."

Now we move on to meet the man who loved and nurtured the Unitarian Society of Wellesley Hills and who created a framework for the congregation it became.

CHAPTER 3

Their First Minister

DIRECTLY OPPOSITE THE Wellesley Unitarian Universalist congregation's chapel and a little to the left near the door is a large plaque that reads, "In memory of Albert Buel Vorse, first minister of this church. He served this people from 1872 until his death in 1899." At the bottom of the plaque is the quotation, "Blessed are the pure in heart." The entire plaque caught my eye when I began as minister of the same church in 1977, partly because there is more than a hint of affection and even deep reverence for Vorse.

Who was this man, and what inspired the devotion inscribed on the plaque? Vorse was born in Lewisburg, Pennsylvania, on November 27, 1831. His father was an attorney, and his mother was a teacher; however, they were apparently not wealthy, as Albert several times had to interrupt his education to earn money, perhaps to help the family. He spent three years at Bucknell University, also in Lewisburg. Vorse studied at a law school in Easton, Pennsylvania, passed the bar, and practiced law for one year.

Eventually Vorse decided he was more suited to ministry. He attended Meadville Theological School, then located in Meadville, Pennsylvania, but left without graduating to become the supply minister of a Unitarian church in Lewisburg. A supply minister fills the pulpit and serves at rites of passage but is not considered the called minister of that congregation. The fact that Vorse took poorly paid ministerial jobs during his education suggests that he did not come from a family of means and struggled to earn the money it took to survive in the ministry. He struggled so much that he could not afford to graduate either from college or theological school.

Vorse's second parish was as supply minister on Cape Cod in Sandwich, Massachusetts, where he met and married Ellen White, the daughter of a prominent citizen of Sandwich. Eventually he was called to Littleton, Massachusetts, where he was ordained and installed in 1863. After serving in Littleton for about six years, he was called to the First Parish of Needham, Massachusetts, in 1871. The story of his then responding to the allure of a bunch of people from Grantville, then known as West Needham, will probably never entirely be known. In an on-line capsule history, the First Parish Needham historian suggests this is the time when they realized they needed to offer their minister more money; in all likelihood, that was Vorse's motivation for jumping ship after less than a year. Albert and Ellen had two children by this time; however, they were leaving an established congregation for a church that was just a gleam in the eyes of maybe forty people.

The person who later wrote Vorse's obituary commented, "How well he performed the duties imposed upon him we all know. He was not only beloved by his parishioners but the whole community loved and esteemed him as a citizen, neighbor, religious teacher and pastor. The memory of his pure, gentle, unselfish life will for years exert an influence for good in this community." The minister of the Hills Congregational Society apparently said, "Every time I meet Rev. Vorse and shake his hand, I feel better for the rest of the day."

Rev. Albert Buel Vorse

Local historian Gamaliel Bradford remembers, "He was quiet, reserved and seemed almost shy. But there was an atmosphere of peculiarly intimate, utterly unpretentious sanctity about him, which impressed even a childhood so indifferent and so erratic as mine."

Rev. Waitstill Sharp wrote a brief history of the founding of the Wellesley Hills church in 1941, perhaps at a time when he had greater access to eyewitness accounts of its founders. He wrote about Albert and Ellen Vorse:

> Rev. and Mrs. Albert Buel Vorse were a team of saints—kindly and pure in heart—gentle spirits whose placid temperaments were needed in the midst of this company of strong willed, vigorous, successful people. . . . It was a friendly providence indeed, which blessed the venture in its opening years with such a pair of ministers—for they were both ministers to the church and to the town. There are varying metals in the foundry where ministers [and their wives] are poured. Had Albert and Ellen Vorse been cast of other metal than they were, there might have been disaster.

They served here from May 5, 1871, until the death of Mr. Vorse in his 68th year on January 21, 1899. To their pastorate goes the credit for the erection of both the present church building and of the parsonage [1891] and the far more significant spiritual building stones—memories of worship, lectures, coffee parties, plays at Shaw Hall, original poems read at dedications of community achievements, social service—twenty-eight years of the precedents of harmony and success, of growth and goodwill and joy in each other.

A long succession of events, unimportant in themselves and transitory, ripens into the most important things of life. Society and societies live by these recollections. Men must believe that something important has happened to them; if they can remember these things together then theirs is the strongest of bonds. This was the gift of Albert and Ellen Vorse for the first twenty-eight years of the church.

The parsonage was then located at the southeast corner of Washington and Forest Streets, just to the right of the former Community Playhouse. The Shaw School stood behind it. Sharp's account continues:

Mrs. Vorse, called 'Auntie' because she was so widely loved by the children, used to leave the rear door of the parsonage open for the Shaw School children to enter for raids upon her famous cookie jar after school. They used to walk in by this back door, help themselves to freshly baked cookies, walked through the house and out the front door. And the front door opened through all those twenty-eight years to friends needing the encouragement of a friendly word, the excitement of talking literature of a winter evening, or an invitation to go blueberrying in the Hundreds.

Albert and Ellen Vorse are remembered for their walking down the streets hand in hand, for their hospitality, for her wit and keen sense of humor and for his gentleness, but chiefly for their unmeasured love of children and their depths of kindliness. Mr. Richard Cunningham relates [1941] that a group of boys about to carry off Mr. Vorse's gate one Hallow'en was deterred by a leader who said, "No, no, we can't play that trick on *him*. He's such a good man." His sermons are remembered by one long observer as "smooth models of English" but his physical frailty forbade any display of power or much emphasis in delivery.

Originally built in 1891 and located on Washington Street, this house served as the USWH parsonage until 1968. As the area became a commercial center, it was moved in 1940 to its present location on Maugus Avenue.

Our Town, published monthly by the town's local ministers and one of the predecessors of the *Wellesley Townsman,* contains one of the few examples of Vorse's writing that is still in print. It is questionable if the descriptor "smooth models of English" applies to this piece. Yet the writer's power of speech and compassion are both clear from the passage and had been clear to his congregation for many years:

On a certain Sunday morning, the rain beating down in the fashion of a driving storm, I stood in a doorway and looked upon a public square in a certain village. The Sunday quiet was upon the scene, and the streets were deserted. As I looked there was only one person crossing the square, an old lady who I was informed had passed her eighty-fifth year. She was very slowly making her way against the storm to her church. . . .

It was an impressive sight; her form was bent with age and her step was feeble. It was clear that something which the storm did not change nor influence was taking her to church where I was told she seldom failed to appear on any Sunday morning of the round year.

And, as I reflected, it seemed quite probable that this presumes something that could prevail upon her to face the discomforts of that walk to her church on such a morning might have had its root in a custom which reached back in the history of her prolonged life. . . . My thoughts said what a wealth of associations had the [custom] brought with it and woven into her heart! Very true it had had its shadow along the way to mingle with the light, just as all kinds of experiences will have. . . . With that company of worshippers with whom she had met from Sunday to Sunday there would be reasons to recall when the sad heart had strength and good cheer poured into it by friends, well tried friends of a common faith, friends united in the spirit of the Master, a source of helpful sympathy that in instances had stood the test and proved unfailing.

Vorse was the right minister for this time for three specific reasons. First, introducing a new Unitarian congregation into a community can create its own mines and snares. As Sharp noted, the Unitarians in Grantville had always been "ground between the upper and the nether millstones of orthodoxy." Apparently the Hills and Village churches were "tight little islands of the saved." The newly-declared Unitarians could have been greeted with a hostility that would have seriously undermined their place in the community.

A story is told in both the Unitarian and Hills Congregational records. A woman who had just moved to Grantville was visited by a delegation of Hills churchwomen. After a tolerable period of small talk the woman rose and said, "It is very kind of you to visit. You know, of course, I am a Universalist." The designated spokeswoman of the Hills delegation responded, "We will come and we will visit you because we like you. But we know that you will not get into heaven!"

A new minister who responded in kind to this sort of interfaith tension would have made the situation intolerably worse. Albert Vorse's response was so disarming that it made friends not only for him and his family but also for the congregation he served. Jonathon Edwards, the Hills Congregational Church minister, gave the prayer at Albert's installation service. When the Reverend Edwards died suddenly, Albert Vorse was out of town. They delayed his memorial service until Albert got back so that he would be able to deliver the eulogy.

A second reason that Vorse was the right minister for this time was his ability to handle thorny situations. Every new congregation's minister has a lot of teaching to do and often teaches to a certain number of people who have no idea how things are done in liberal congregations. What they particularly do not know is how to handle divisions as they arise and how to deal with divisive personalities who could split the congregation. The story of Rev. Vorse conducting a service of dedication without actually calling it one in order to resolve a conflict peacefully demonstrates that when his benevolent presence passed over a potentially rancorous situation, the rancor often vanished.

Third, it is not every minister who likes children or gets on well with them. In fact many clergy of that era were almost indifferent to all but their own children. Yet the Vorses absolutely loved children, and that went a long way toward an atmosphere in the congregation and throughout the town that made the Unitarian church seem like a valuable addition to the community.

Albert Vorse died of a malignancy on his neck on January 21, 1899. A parishioner who reported his funeral wrote:

> His quiet influence has made a deep impression on the community no one can doubt who saw the large gathering filling the Unitarian church gather to give silent expression to the strong regard in which all held this pure and earnest man. . . .
>
> As they passed in mute farewell, all must have felt how peaceful was the rest of such a soul even as the quiet of his body resting among the flowers he loved, all tributes from loving friends.

CHAPTER 4

Getting Started

EXCERPTS FROM STANDING Committee and congregational meetings records detail the events leading up to the Grantville Unitarians building their first real church building.

At the annual meeting of 1878, the treasurer reported that the congregation had no outstanding debts but had no money in the treasury. In response, the Reverend Vorse announced that if it would help, he would be happy to give back some part of his salary. The congregation was taken by surprise at this announcement. Wondering if their minister was blaming himself for his congregation not turning a surplus, they voted a unanimous expression of confidence in him and told him he could contribute a portion of his salary or not, and they would be equally happy.

The minister's salary remained at $1,500 each year for the rest of his tenure. Perhaps they thought that if he received an increase he would just try to return it. If that were true perhaps his wife Ellen would have made a remark similar to that made by the wife of the Lutheran minister in a sketch by Garrison Keillor. The minister in question had just turned back the money they had set aside for their family vacation in Florida. His wife said to him, "You may have noticed that all of the great martyrs of history went to their doom alone. They didn't take their wives and family with them."

In the April 1879 annual report, a tribute appeared to one of their founders who had died that year. A tribute appeared every time one of their number died. One tribute read, "Resolved that in the death of our brother, David C. Perrin, our church has lost a firm friend, a modest man, a hearty coworker and a worthy Christian associate whose memory we shall long cherish."

The same annual report discusses repairs that had to be made to the chapel. The moderator began the discussion by saying, "Although there was some difference of opinion about it," still he trusted that "it could be discussed in the true Christian spirit." In 1880 after laying out $500 for more repairs to the roof, treasurer Rebecca Eaton noted that she feels "confident that we could not have made a better investment for $500" and she is "for the first time more hopeful for the coming year than we were for the last." She thinks few if any would go back to "the leaky roof, stained walls, and forlorn aspect of things a few years ago."

In 1882 the same treasurer reported that while the Society had an empty treasury, it is free of debt and the past year had been marked by an unusual degree of unanimity and activity. In 1883 it was noted that the chapel lawn had become a playground because the gates were left open. In 1884 a resolution asked if the congregation would approve the use of the front lawn of the chapel for tennis games. It was decided that the rear of the property would be more appropriate for that purpose.

The congregation also voted in 1884 to hold quarterly meetings in January, April, July, and October. We can only guess at why they chose to do this. Perhaps they were keenly aware that as a small congregation they could be seriously hurt if a small group of people felt they had been ignored or overridden and walked off in anger.

Frequently decisions were tabled or deferred simply because the people present did not feel comfortable making a decision that might upset others.

In 1886 the Standing Committee reported it was looking at area churches that had been built recently with seating for about 200. The notation read, "It was thought that this size church might answer for the present but not for the future. The preaching of liberal Christianity here for the last fifteen years has so modified the theological tone of the people that a larger and better church is demanded." It was moved and unanimously voted that a committee "of six ladies" be appointed to see how much "material aid can be secured within our own midst towards building a new church."

Over the course of two years, they solicited and received for review several architectural plans. One of them was by Shaw and Hunnewell. The Hunnewell might have been Hollis Hunnewell who, though not a member of the church, contributed $5,000 to the new building. The Shaw was probably founding church member John W. Shaw, a generous real estate broker. The duo envisioned a sanctuary with seating for 250 and a parlor both for informal gathering and for use in case of overflow congregations, probably the size of the present chapel, with folding doors and seating for 150.

In June of 1887 the congregation voted to send what they hoped were final plans, this time by architects Rotch and Tilden, to Hollis Hunnewell for his approval per the request he made when he promised a $5,000 contribution. The Honorable J.G. Abbott donated boulders for the church walls from his property in the Cliff Road area, and John Shaw donated the bell among other things.

While the walls of the new building were rising above the ground, the congregation put the Maugus Hall "chapel" up for auction. Meanwhile they accepted the offer of the Hills Congregational Church to use their sanctuary on Sunday afternoons until the new church was built.

The new building was dedicated on November 20, 1888. It was apparently "a beautiful day and a large attendance numbering in round numbers 400 people." The net cost of the church was $18,288.12.

New USWH stone church constructed in 1888

According to the reporter who covered the event for the *Courant*, another predecessor of the *Wellesley Townsman*, the sermon by the Reverend Brooke Hereford "was a very forcible and direct statement of the utility of church organization and the duty of personal attendance on public worship as incumbent on each individual." Sometimes the guest preacher customarily asks the incumbent minister if he has any preference as to what his congregation hears. Perhaps this sermon topic reflected Albert Vorse's request or possibly Brooke Hereford's personal peeve. The *Courant* article continues:

> The new building has a seating capacity for 250 persons but by use of settees and the parlor which faces the pulpit directly an audience of 400 can be easily accommodated. The architects, Messers Rotch and Tilden, have been very successful in presenting a structure that is massive, imposing and ornamental, though in this they are

somewhat restricted by the moderate limits of the building fund. This led to a simplicity of construction and the use of boulders from the neighboring fields for building stone which gives a certain dignity to the edifice, which would easily be lost in any attempt to make a small building an imitation of a large one.

An impression of solidity is given by the massive masonry and the broad spreading slate roof relieved by a picturesque belfry recalling the small churches of Normandy. The chief aim of the architects has been to avoid anything like imitation and pretense but rather to furnish a simple, solid and substantial structure ornamental to the village and of permanent utility to the occupants. The same directness of construction is observed in the interior, where the roof is open to the ridgepole with stained natural woods for the slips, chancel and dado. High decorated screen work on either side of the platform encloses the minister's room and the organ.

Interior of new church built in 1888

The interior is typical of late nineteenth-century churches: pulpit in the center of the church at the front, with minister's room and organ on either side. Since ministers then were thought to work and counsel at home, the minister's room in those days was probably a robe room for the minister before the service. Many organs were later moved from the front to the balcony in the back where the organist could direct the choir to the best acoustic advantage.

It might be difficult for us to imagine now how proud the members were of this new building, finished and dedicated just fourteen years after they had formally begun. Treasurer Rebecca Eaton reported:

> The building of this church which was thought by some to be a doubtful experiment has proved to be a decided success. There is a debt of $4,000 on the building, which will not be a burden to the Society. . . . The present condition of the church is hopeful. If we can carry on the same unanimity that has characterized the society to a remarkable degree in the past into the future, a strong and active church must be the result.

Building a new parsonage proved to be a momentary break in this reign of harmony. Why the congregation wanted a new parsonage is not recorded anywhere. The old parsonage was conveniently located nearby at the corner of Forest and Washington Streets. The Vorse family had not increased its numbers necessitating a new house. In fact, over three or four months of Standing Committee meetings during which there were a number of inconclusive exchanges and seemingly heated debate, no opinion was recorded from the occupants of the old parsonage. Whatever the reason, the fate of the minister's accommodations hung in the balance for about half a year.

In those days and until comparatively recently, ministers of New England congregations were not invited to meetings of the governing board. In 1969 when I signaled my intention to attend my first meeting of the parish board of the First Parish of Canton, Massachusetts, the board had to decide whether or not to break with tradition and allow the board meetings to proceed with benefit of clergy. One reason for this practice might have been that ministers were thought to be wholly unrealistic about business matters, and their contributions would only muddy up the discussion. Or perhaps many New England parishioners did not want their ministers involved in the political or economic life of the congregation. Ministers' involvement might entangle them too much in how things really worked, and they might discover which members paid the larger part of the bill.

Some of the lots under consideration for the new parsonage were owned either by church members or by friends of members, which may have been a partial source of the controversy. A lot across the street from the church on Maugus Avenue facing the church was chosen. Much later the house built on that lot was turned to face Maugus Avenue and remained the parsonage partway through the ministry of Bill Rice.

The parish meeting of 1890 turned out to be a time when some of the founders began to step back from their heavy responsibilities. In addition, Louisa Eaton Austin, who had been the organist since the beginning, also stepped down from that position. The Standing Committee passed a resolution thanking her, but at the annual meeting it was suggested that the previous resolution had been too mild in its praise, and a more vigorous one was passed. One explanation might be that there were some in the congregation who had begun to think a new and better-trained hand at the organ keyboard was in order and had perhaps pushed this resignation a bit.

On July 6, 1890, Rebecca Eaton and John Shaw were delegated to decide whether to keep the church open during the summer. At the same time, it was announced that Mr. Vorse's vacation would run from mid-July through August. If the church were to be kept open all summer, the services would have to be conducted by guest preachers who would have to be paid. The Wellesley Hills Unitarian Society then followed the practice, not only of other Unitarian churches in the

Boston area but of other Wellesley churches of several denominations, of not holding worship services through much of the summer.

This no-summer-services practice began early in nineteenth-century New England when many people associated dread summertime diseases such as polio with air and waterborne carriers. Many felt that large cities like Boston and its immediate environs were not healthy places particularly for children to be. Hence families took off for the summer to cottages in Maine, New Hampshire, the Massachusetts south shore, and Cape Cod. The proliferation of railroads even made it possible for wage earners to commute every day from their summer cottages to Boston. Since the churches of the well-to-do were virtually empty on summer Sunday mornings, ministers were given most of July and August as vacation. This summer break became an expectation for both ministers and their congregations that has lasted much longer than the threat of summer diseases.

In 1977 a local Wellesley minister said, "If you really want a quiet summer for reading and writing, stay here in town. There's nobody here. They've all gone." That may have been true then; however, it is no longer the case. Perhaps this is because summer homes are expensive to keep or even rent, and the diseases once associated with city life are now avoidable or treatable. Fewer people leave, and those who are around are looking for opportunities to gather with their chosen congregations.

On April 29, 1891, Rebecca Eaton marked the twentieth anniversary of the congregation as follows:

> The Twentieth Anniversary of an organization needs something more than mere figures. In twenty years we have come to our annual meeting with every bill for current expenses paid, and it is a record that we may well be proud of.

What has been accomplished thus far has been entirely by the principle of voluntary contribution, each one contributing every year just what he thinks he can afford. No one knowing what anyone else gives and the giver of the smallest sum or even he who can't afford to give anything having just as good a right and just as good a piece as he who gives the largest sum.

The voluntary system was a prominent feature of the organization of the church and twenty years' experience proves that it has been successful. It was felt that there should be one place at least where there was no money distinction, and it has been no doubt the source of no small satisfaction to those who have been able to give liberally for the support of the church to feel that their less favored friends have enjoyed through their liberality the same advantages with themselves.

The Ladies Sewing Circle has been quite an important aid to the church not only in raising money but in affording the opportunity for all to contribute their full share. Those who cannot give money can here give an equivalent and it tends to deepen the interest in the church where each one feels that he is doing his part towards its support.

Aside from the pecuniary aid which this circle has rendered we could ill afford to lose the social life and strength that it has afforded. True, in all these years we have had discouragements. We have lost by death and by removals many tried and valued friends. One year the subscription sheet would show only eighteen names, but faith and zeal know no such words as fail, and now with about forty subscribers and a steady gain every year, is not the forward look a helpful one? Let us then each and all do our part towards hastening the day when a strong and vigorous church and a church free from debt can open its doors to all alike and shall be a fixed fact in Wellesley Hills.

In fact, growth was already happening. Average attendance was forty out of a membership of a little over eighty. The church school listed forty-six pupils. The choir had seventeen active members. A lending library contained 345 books—larger than many small town public libraries.

At this twentieth celebration those gathered sang an original hymn by Mary C. Smith to the tune of "Auld Lang Syne":

> *We meet tonight to tell our love, a love both sweet and strong.*
> *For this dear Mother Church, which holds us tenderly and long.*
> *For twenty years have passed away, since first we sought her side.*
> *And still she draws us to her heart. May peace with her abide.*
> *We sing the faith of him who led this band, in numbers small.*
> *Yet strong to do and brave to bear all trials which befall.*
>
> *We sing the hope, which kept their hearts.*
> *They fainted not nor failed.*
> *We sing of love. Round one and all it bound a golden chain.*
> *We gladly welcome all who come, our power to renew.*
> *We whisper soft of many a one now vanished from our view.*
> *And so we sing, let voices ring, our love so deep and strong.*
> *God bless our Church grant she still holds us tenderly and long.*

Attending this service were several ministers who had spoken twenty years ago at the dedication of the Society and the chapel, which had been Maugus Hall. Also speaking were the ministers of the Hills and the Village Congregational churches who expressed their appreciation at having been invited and their feeling that the Society had become a full and valued part of the Wellesley community of faiths.

The hymn was followed by a poem to the Sewing Circle. Finally, there were brief words by Mr. Vorse who "in a tender and most feeling manner . . . reviewed his pastorate and the dedication services held twenty years ago in which the Reverend James Freeman Clarke preached the sermon, Professor Young gave him the Charge, and the Reverend J. E. Folsom extended the right hand of fellowship to him. He spoke of members who have rendered the Society much help and of the worthiness of Miss Rebecca Eaton to whom the church owes much gratitude. After singing a hymn the remainder of the evening was devoted to social intercourse and collation."

When all the good fellowship of that evening had passed, financial issues still remained. The finance committee reported that their subscription [pledge] drive had yielded only half what was needed. This left three options: borrow from the American Unitarian Association and thus be listed on their rolls as "missionary work"; appeal to persons outside the church who had been generous in the past; or conduct a fair. They chose the third option and charged the "ladies" to conduct a fair. Although it did not erase the entire deficit, the fair left them with the feeling that they could live with whatever money they had.

At the annual meeting of 1892, there was a discussion about the allotment of pews. It seemed as if there were more families attending more or less regularly than there were pews. The practice of the Society had been to hold a lottery once a year during which every family would draw a number. The family with number one would choose their pew first and so on in numerical order. Next year a new lottery would be held so that families who were unhappy with their previous location in the church were given the chance to improve their situation. The alternative of asking pew rentals of each family was disapproved by the congregation's tradition and by the American Unitarian Association. Apparently the present system of first come, first seated wherever they want to sit was either not considered or it was deemed too terribly radical to be raised.

CHAPTER 5

Ongoing Concerns

NEARLY EVERY PARISH board encounters the usual kinds of brush fires to put out. Following are some issues that came up frequently at monthly and annual meetings of the church between 1871 and 1899.

Finances: Even though they were never seriously in debt during this period, the church skated very close to the line. Several committees complained frequently that their budget should not always take the hit during lean times. With few exceptions members of this congregation were not wealthy nor did they live in an extraordinarily wealthy community as might be deemed the case today.

Democracy: The congregation worked very hard—frequently postponing decisions over several meetings—so that everyone concerned could participate and be heard. Many of the elected leaders seemed to have been strong-minded individuals who were used to getting their way in other venues but submitted to the caretaking of the congregation's democratic process.

Church school: During this period, the church school grew from twenty or thirty to ninety scholars, as they called them. Yet religious education often ran short of funds. When many of the founding members of the congregation went to church with their parents, they probably sat through the entire service and got whatever there was to be gotten from sermons preached entirely to adults. Church school was a new idea, but many of this congregation's parents took it seriously and made sure that the congregation regularly supported the Unitarian Sunday School Society which advocated progressive religious education.

Maintenance: For a congregation that was barely twenty to twenty-five years old, they owned a lot of real estate, and it was expensive to keep up.

Real Estate: Church property backs up to the Worcester Turnpike and the Boston & Albany Railroad. A path from the church to the Turnpike was paved. In the early years, final property boundaries had to be negotiated and determined.

View of USWH from atop Maugus Hill

Music: Occasionally the church could sustain a choir of around seventeen singers; more often they paid for a quartet, which seemed to please most people. The music salaries would have included the quartet singers, the organist/choir director, and a "boy to blow the organ" as they put it. This meant a boy was needed to work large bellows that forced air through the organ pipes while it was being played. As in any congregation there were surely those who loved the deep mellow sounds of the organ; others thought they could readily do without the expense of it and would be very happy with a piano as the church musical accompaniment. The music program was expensive but apparently a priority of most, for it kept being funded.

Attendance: Although slowly but steadily improving during the first twenty-five years of this church's story, attendance was continually a concern. In 1899 the Standing Committee wrote in its annual report:

> In common with some other parishes of different denominations we have to lament the indifference to public worship and general religious work of many members who profess our faith and especially of most of the young men. Whatever are the reasons for this it works a hardship upon others and endangers church, society and government. Clergymen often lamented the evil but have almost ceased to preach about it, because recognizing it and advertising it causes many to regard it as popular. But we speak as laymen, possibly in some measure guilty ourselves, and we are impelled to say that in our opinion this Society, notwithstanding its good start, its considerable investment of property, its beautiful buildings and its flourishing Sunday school is in danger of dissolution and decay unless young men become responsible for its success.
>
> Doubtless they have not realized this danger nor what it would mean to our town, to the value of property here, to our denomination and to the cause of Christianity.

Although this was written shortly after the death of Albert Vorse, a time during which attendance may well have fallen off, attendance was a constant concern to members of the congregation. Perhaps they had no way of knowing that clergymen had noted the absence of young men and the decline of regular attendance ever since the end of Puritanism, more than a century and a half earlier.

It was during this time that Frank and Lucy Baldwin became active in the church and enrolled their children in the church school. According to the biography written of their eldest son Roger, they were not "regular church goers." They told Roger they were "agnostic Unitarians." Although this description today would have described many Unitarian Universalists in every church, in those days it probably reflected that they felt some distance from the members of the congregation who were largely liberal Christian.

Nonetheless, Frank and Lucy Baldwin regularly took their children to church school, and their names appeared on committees and at annual meetings. They did both resign during the troubled latter years of John Snyder. Even so, according to Roger's biography by Robert Cottrell:

> The Unitarian church served as Roger's social center; he even taught Sunday school there. Little concerned about questions of immortality, he developed an "unquestioning belief in man if not God." While still a youngster he rejected atheism, reasoning that some ethereal force held the universe together. Such a force also suggested the possibility that striving for a common good was a worthwhile endeavor. As a teenager Roger was attracted to the works of Jesus whom he revered "not as a divine figure but for what he said." Roger participated in the social service efforts of the Unitarian church including its Lend a Hand Society, founded by Edward Everett Hale. The nonsectarian organization was identified with the motto, "Look up, not down. Look forward and not back. Look out and not in, and lend a hand."

Roger Baldwin later became the director of the American Civil Liberties Union and a pioneer in that cause.

Church founding member and long-time treasurer Rebecca Eaton died in 1897. The following tribute written into the minutes of that year reflects a good deal of what the church had valued in their time together as well as what they gained from her presence among them:

> In the death of Miss Rebecca Eaton, we lose from this church and community a most efficient aid in every good cause. She was by nature endowed for making her life one of noble influence and strength to the world about her. Her qualities of mind and heart made for her the place she came to fill and she nobly gave herself to it.
>
> She was faithful in all things. Her life was a notable instance of the faithful life. A true child of our Unitarian faith, she was its loyal advocate in her quiet though exemplary and efficient manner of making its principles known and understood. Miss Eaton was one of the original founders of our church; to her, in great measure, may be traced the inspiration of the movement through all of its early struggles for permanent and growing life. In all of these years of its further history it has had her force of character, her judicial counsel, her active energy and her capable devotion to its interests. She gave herself freely to years of constant and active labor in its behalf. In the management of its affairs she naturally was chosen to office, but she needed no incentive of this nature to call her interest and aid; that was always present and alive, for it had the source of a devotion that was constant and of the heart. With this so very true of her all things needful to be done had her attention and aid. With talent for doing well in what was greatest she was equally ready to serve in what was least. Her memory will be fondly cherished by a grateful people who having known her worth esteemed and loved her as only the good and true are loved and esteemed.

Albert Buel Vorse, the other great pillar of the congregation, died on January 21, 1899, at the age of sixty-eight after a twenty-eight-year ministry. The Standing Committee noted they are told this was one of the longest incumbencies of the denomination at that time. He saw the Society grow from forty members to 116. He buried nearly all of the founding members and yet seemed to welcome many new members with equal regard. "His quiet dignity, his loving spirit, and the even tenor of his way were influences in a changing parish, which cannot be lightly estimated," wrote a parishioner. As is true in many such situations, he had been "the church" for many, and now it was time for members to test themselves on the next phase of their journey.

CHAPTER 6

Their First Serious Test

THE LOSS OF a beloved, long-tenured minister—no matter how much anticipated—can be devastating for a congregation. It is a time when some members wonder if their allegiance to the church can survive the loss of their minister. Inevitably there are some who conclude that it will not, and so they resign or, more likely, quietly slip away—decreasing their pledges and becoming more absent on Sunday mornings. Under the best of circumstances, they know there will be a new—and unknown—spiritual leader setting the tone for worship.

Around the turn of the century, the procedure for finding a new minister was that the congregation's governing board was authorized to compile a list of ministers they would like to consider. Many ministers would take the initiative to throw their names into the hat as soon as possible. The board would then invite those ministers to preach and conduct worship in their own church over a series of Sundays after which the congregation would vote its preferences. In an informal ballot at 7:30 p.m. on October 17, 1899, the Wellesley Hills congregation cast five votes for Mr. Mott, three votes for Mr. Jones, one vote for Mr. Pettingill, twenty-seven votes for Mr. Snyder, and twenty-eight votes for Mr. Pratt.

After considerable discussion and a reading of the references for the leading candidates, another informal vote was taken: thirty-six votes for Mr. Snyder and twenty-six votes for Mr. Pratt. At this point a formal vote was taken: fifty-one votes for Mr. Snyder and two for Mr. Pratt. The Reverend John M. Snyder was elected. But did he ever learn that at one point there were more people against him than for him? And what did it mean to members of the congregation that John Snyder was not the undisputed first choice to be their next minister?

On paper Rev. Snyder would have been an easy pick. In December of 1899, he was described as "a man of middle age and a genial personality who has attained a high position in the Unitarian denomination." Born in Philadelphia on June 14, 1842, he enlisted in the Union Army in 1861 and was given a command. But after several months' service he became sick and spent a long time in army hospitals before he was discharged in 1862.

Snyder entered Meadville Theological School in 1865 and graduated in 1869. At that time he became minister of the Third Unitarian Church in Hingham, Massachusetts. In 1873 he became minister of the Church of the Messiah in St. Louis where he enjoyed a long pastorate of twenty-six years. He was "an able and exceedingly popular minister; no minister being better known in that city." Under his leadership a "new and beautiful church, one of the finest and certainly the most beautiful of the city" was erected. During this time he was also a trustee of the American Unitarian Association and Meadville Theological School. He met and married Margaret Kinniff of Meadville, Pennsylvania, and they became the parents of nine children.

Snyder was described in the Wellesley newspaper as "in the full vigor of his powers, and a most interesting preacher, a most social and companionable man, a lover of children who always return his love, a genial and friendly disposition whose heart never harbors an unkind feeling toward any living soul."

At the Unitarian Church in St. Louis, Snyder followed the Reverend William Greenleaf Eliot who was such a fixture in the Midwest that he was often called the "Unitarian Bishop," since he traveled far and wide to spread the cause of religious liberalism. Thus, Snyder was no stranger to following a man like Albert Vorse who many of his parishioners considered a Unitarian saint.

What the Wellesley congregation could not have known at the time is that John Snyder had been the minister in place while the future poet T. S. Eliot was a child in his congregation. In a biography of the young Eliot, Robert Crawford suggests that Snyder had both positive and negative influences on the man who later became one of the twentieth century's best-known poets. Snyder was a conservative and intellectual Christian who believed that our duty in life is to live as piously and virtuously as did Jesus. His sermons, based on his understanding of the Bible and on New England poets, suggested Christianity was very important and that the early Unitarians were the original Christians following the teachings of Jesus unadorned by Trinitarian doctrinal trappings.

As the young Eliot grew into early adulthood, he realized that John Snyder's Christian identification was very important to him as well but that Unitarianism would not remain in that Christian camp much longer. Eliot also realized that Rev. Snyder's optimism about men and women achieving a state of virtue without the aid of a divine Christ was something he could not share.

To gain a closer look at John Snyder, following is a passage he wrote for the December 1900 issue of *Our Town*, a newspaper edited by the Wellesley clergy:

Society really makes no allowances for the curious paradoxes of self-deception. Every man is regarded as a simple hypocrite whose moral life is out of harmony with his religious profession.

Therefore we may agree with Paul in his feeling that religion demands ourselves rather than our possessions or our activities. Religion demands self-consecration and will be satisfied with nothing less. How then do we respond to this demand? A little trace of hedonism remains with us yet. . . . The religious faith demands a personal priesthood. It asks for personal service and will be satisfied with no vicarious sacrifice [possibly a reference to Christ's sacrifice on the cross for humanity's sins]. . . .

Must a small devoted minority do the work of making the world a better place to live in? Are you willing to enjoy the fruits of their consecrated labor and do nothing to add to the common [good]?

Snyder goes on to say that the religious institutions of the town make "more secure the welfare of every household and yet a large percentage of its men withhold from such institutions not their money but what no money can purchase—the precious wealth of personal service."

Although he may have had a genial disposition, Snyder was awfully hard on himself and on other people. He expected great things from his congregation and from himself. His ministry followed that of Albert Buel Vorse, a gentle grandfatherly spirit whose only strong wish was that his parishioners be happy—not necessarily perfect. It often happens that congregations in search tend to look first for qualities that their beloved previous minister did not have. Albert Buel Vorse was a pastor first, and all other qualities came second. John Snyder was a Christian preacher and teacher first, and other qualities came second.

Snyder started out with a sermon series on "The Great Figures of the Bible." Shortly thereafter he preached a series on the great figures

of Genesis. Most of his sermons were Biblically based, and they may
have been somewhat more like
lectures that the sermons
Wellesley parishioners were used
to hearing. For example, one
sermon's title was "Things in the
Parables That Are Hard to
Understand." One year his Easter
sermon was titled "How May We
Perfect the Lives of the Saints?"

Snyder was determined to
grow this church with what had
worked for him in the Midwest.
He sponsored a lecture series on

Rev. John M. Snyder

Unitarianism in the Wellesley Town Hall. Keynote speaker for the
first night was Samuel Atkins Eliot II, president of the American
Unitarian Association. On Sundays after the service, he held a well-
attended class on the origins of Christianity at the parsonage. When
it was noted there were a number of Wellesley College students in the
sanctuary on Sundays, several people thought it would be nice if they
could have the college addresses of the students who were listed as
Unitarians so that they could make it possible for all to attend services.
They asked, and the college refused to provide them.

No doubt some of Snyder's efforts bore fruit in attracting new
people. The yearly statistics suggested that the congregation was
growing slowly both in adults and children. In addition, the weekly
paper announced that John Snyder was off lecturing at another
Unitarian church six or more times each month, so it seemed that he
was thought to be an entertaining fellow who was worth listening to.
But there were other signs that were a little bit disquieting. Pledges
had fallen off in 1901 and 1902; there was some worry about whether

the Society would be able to pay its bills. There was much concern about children who were no longer showing up in Sunday school. A number of people resigned from committee leadership, and the Standing Committee had to recruit new leadership continually.

Committees began to fight with one another, and the Standing Committee asked "the pastor" to meet with the combatants and try to settle things down. The fact that this became necessary may have caused people to recall—accurately or not—that Vorse never missed a committee meeting whereas Snyder did not seem to attend them.

Perhaps a partial hint to the problem is in this announcement in the January 1903 issue of *Our Town*: "The Unitarian Club of the church held a discussion on 'How Shall I Use Sunday.' Several spoke followed by questions from the pastor. Twenty-five members responded." The next meeting was on "The Duties of the Layman to the Church." This February presentation was followed by "a lively and *frank* [emphasis added] discussion." We have no witness still living to tell us whether this was an airing of concerns, but it seems so. It was shortly after this meeting that Snyder preached on perfecting the lives of the saints.

There were considerable difficulties with the Sunday school, and Snyder was asked to step in and provide some leadership. Pledge revenues were falling off, and the finance committee began to wonder if there was a better way to raise money for the church. In 1904 they adopted the equivalent of an every-member canvass, something they had not tried rigorously before this. John Snyder did have ideas about membership, but they were more along the lines of asking new members to subscribe to a bond of union. This idea, now called a "covenant," is proposed in many congregations today. It still runs into the objections of some that it sounds like being asked to swear loyalty to a creed—something they thought that Unitarians would never do.

In the 1903 annual meeting, Rev. John Snyder made three recommendations: that a member of the Standing Committee be appointed to be particularly concerned with helping move attendees into membership and then into making a financial commitment; that a member of the Standing Committee be placed on the Sunday school committee; and that a committee be organized to confer with him about the formation of a religious bond of union for those who wished to make joining the congregation a public religious [statement.] He was politely given the chance to speak and make proposals, but then the meeting followed the order of the warrant for the meeting. No discussion is recorded or vote taken.

In the Midwest where Snyder spent twenty-six years in ministry, these ideas would have found acceptance at least among some in the congregation; a committee to write a religious bond would have been formed. But this was New England, and very possibly John Snyder had not been there long enough to have his suggestions taken seriously— even on a highly concerning matter such as the commitments of new members.

Going into the year 1904, the Standing Committee decided that the best way of raising money to support the church was to canvass each member personally, explain the dire financial situation of the church, and then ask for a 25–50% pledge increase. Amazingly this worked, and with variations in the pitch it worked for several more years.

In 1905, Snyder brought his own play titled "As Ye Sow" to the Boston stage. He had written it earlier and brought it to the Chicago stage where it did very well. According to a *Boston Daily Globe* review, he was "the first American clergyman who has written a successful play." The *Globe* review continued:

> [Rev. John Snyder] came here from St. Louis where he spent many years as a contributor to the daily papers and magazines. He has written a number of stories the most recent one being "The Wind Trust", a sociological study. But "As Ye Sow" is his first experiment in dramatic literature.

Speaking of the inspiration for his play the other day, Rev. Snyder said, "The initial incentive for 'As Ye Sow' was my desire to see a wholesome, normal minister presented upon the stage. I thought it due to my profession that it ought not to be continually misrepresented on the stage by characters who do not begin to suggest the typical clergyman.

I have always attended the theatre because I believe the stage is the most powerful medium for the inculcation of all the great moral thoughts and that the stage gives the most impressive utterance to the great principles of life. I was therefore familiar with most of the stage ministers before I started to write my play."

Snyder goes on in this interview to explain that he was talking with a friend who was a professional actor about his disagreement with the way in which ministers were generally portrayed in the theater. His friend suggested that he write a play representing the clergyman figure as he thought he should be presented. Snyder said, "I was very pleased with the way clergymen in Chicago heartily approved of my treatment of our profession on the stage." A *Boston Globe* drama critic described the play:

It is a simple human presentation of human passion in which the good man and the selfish man reap the kind of harvest they have sowed and nothing else. . . . It fairly bristles with stirring situations and it possesses an abundance of boisterous comedy. This is thoroughly enjoyable.

The scenes are laid on Cape Cod and the dramatist has been very successful in suggesting local atmosphere in the surroundings amid which his cleverly drawn characters appear. . . .

The critical character is a sturdy young minister, the embodiment of all human virtues. He loved a young woman who "has a past." She believes herself however to be a widow as she consents to marry the minister. Just at the moment they are about to be married a great storm bursts forth. [We are told] that a ship is rapidly approaching destruction on the rocks of a nearby coast. The ceremony is interrupted, and the minister forms one of a volunteer lifesaving crew who rescues the drowning sailors. One of the rescued proved to be not only the husband of the woman who was about to be married to the minister but also the long lost brother of the same minister.

Unpleasant complications naturally ensue. The returned brother is the most villainous sort of rascal imaginable and during two acts he makes everybody miserable by his unjust suspicions of the entirely virtuous couple, who sacrifice to him all of their desires.

In the end he goes away and a discriminating Spanish bullet opens the way for future happiness for his widow and his brother.

While it is not known how long "As Ye Sow" played in Boston, it played to highly appreciative audiences. A group of London clergy invited the cast and author to present the play in London. Since there was no town newspaper for Wellesley in 1905, there is no way to tell how the news of Snyder's success was received locally. There is no mention of it either directly or by implication in either Standing Committee minutes or the records of the annual meeting.

From the latter part of 1905 to 1908, many members of the church leadership seemed to have a "glass half empty" perspective on the church. The membership actually had grown thirty percent in ten years, but the Standing Committee groused that not all of them were attending regularly and not all of those who were attending were members. The church school grew from fifty-two to eighty-nine students during the same period, and the average attendance more than doubled. A choir formed, funded by special donations, which members greatly appreciated.

A special fundraising letter went out to the larger donors, and the results were fairly rewarding. Hence they decided to send a similar letter out to other members asking their advice concerning finances.

By the annual meeting of 1907, the Standing Committee declared the year had been "a quiet one"; however, the Sunday school had grown to 114 students. There was a clear lack of volunteers, and the minister was asked to make a plea from the pulpit for more people to help with the work of the congregation. By January of 1908 they decided to call a congregational meeting to present the problem of fewer volunteers. This tends to be a losing strategy since most people do not react well to being scolded or to being asked to do what they are told no one else wants to do. In March of 1908 the estimated deficit was $300, a real cause for concern. A letter was sent to attempt to make up the deficit by special donations.

In September the Standing Committee agreed it should meet with Snyder, and in October a special meeting of the congregation was called. At this time Snyder read his letter of resignation. Although we do not have a copy of it, the following was written: "Mr. Snyder said he thought it best that no public announcement of his resignation be made as the Standing Committee would be overrun with applications. He said he had arranged to exchange with candidates and that the Standing Committee would go to the 'Unitarian rooms' [apparently headquarters back then] and under the advice of the officers select any accredited minister they wished and he would arrange to exchange with them."

At this distance in time and with as no written testimonies from parishioners about the causes of the upset, it is difficult to know what the bill of complaint against Rev. John Snyder was. The congregation, young and old, increased during his years of ministry, and Snyder's stature as a minister of considerable standing also increased. Even so, it is very difficult to follow a long-tenured minister, because much that the new minister preaches or does reminds people that the beloved former minister did it differently.

The *Wellesley Townsman*, the town's new newspaper that began publishing in 1906, carried no announcement of Snyder's departure. The *Boston Globe* published a column on December 13, 1908, announcing that he had accepted a call to the Unitarian Church at Nantucket. After explaining that in addition to being a minister he had been a successful playwright, the column ended with these words: "His resignation here was received with much regret. Under his direction the Wellesley Hills church had grown rapidly into one of the most flourishing parishes of the Unitarian faith in this vicinity."

CHAPTER 7

The Perils and Promise of Growth

LOCAL HISTORIAN ELIZABETH Hinchcliffe wrote in her centennial history of Wellesley:

> Wellesley had come very far very quickly reaching a population of 6400 by 1915. There were those who approved; there were those who didn't.
>
> Wellesley was still a town of dichotomies. The most modern inventions co-existed with farmers and tramps who made their way through town knocking at back doors. Steam engines and electric cars covered the landscape. . . . *Our Town*, the local newspaper that continued through into the early 1900s, was filled with articles defending or attacking Wellesley's growth.

While some Wellesley residents were rather grumpy about the effects of modernization, others were euphoric. Growth in a community tends to benefit its religious institutions if they have a minister who seems to be in tune with the interests of the people moving in.

In April 1909, however, church school attendance had fallen from sixty-five to less than thirty. The choir had shrunk to a quartet after the director had left for Utah. The church and parsonage badly needed repairs. And the minister had resigned. A pulpit committee formed to recommend a new candidate. This would be a very important choice.

The first candidate split the votes of those who heard him right down the middle. A motion to employ him on a trial basis for a year and four months was defeated. The pulpit committee then voted to ask him to preach to the entire congregation on a Sunday in order to get their opinion. Apparently the reaction was negative. The committee then offered the call to two or three more candidates—one of whom was a Harvard student at the time and went on to have a very successful career in the Unitarian ministry. All three turned Wellesley down. Finally, they offered the job to the Reverend William H. Ramsay of the Church of the Messiah [Unitarian] in Louisville, Kentucky.

A news clipping from the American Unitarian Association's *Christian Register* datelined December 31, 1909, Church of the Messiah, Louisville, Kentucky, read:

> The trustees have received the resignation of Rev. William H. Ramsay who for the past seven years has held the pastorate of that church. Mr. Ramsay is now at Boston and when he left Louisville several days ago it was understood that his resignation would be forwarded from that city although the fact was not made known to any but the trustees.
>
> The news of Mr. Ramsay's resignation will be received with great regret by members of his church with whom he is very popular as well as by the citizens of Louisville at large who have observed his labors for a better Louisville.
>
> Since coming to this city Mr. Ramsay has always taken a deep interest in public education and has always preached a number of sermons on our public schools which made a lasting impression. He

was the first vice president of the Anti-Tuberculosis Association and has served as a member of the Board of Children's Guardians. Mr. Ramsay is a man of wide culture. The primary reason for prompting Mr. Ramsay's resignation is the fact that his daughter will enter college in Boston and both he and Mrs. Ramsay wish to relocate near that city for this reason.

A January 21 *Wellesley Townsman* article reported that Ramsay was born in Ireland fifty years ago and was educated for ministry in the Methodist Episcopal Church in Belfast. Before ordination he found himself becoming more liberal and entered Harvard Divinity School in 1895. In 1889 he married Miss Katherine Pierson of Salem, and in 1892 they became parents of one child named Margaret.

In 1896 Ramsay was ordained as a Unitarian minister in Salem, Massachusetts. He then served a congregation in Colorado and later moved to Middleboro, Massachusetts, where he built a successful church. From there he went to Manchester, New Hampshire, for two years and then to Farmington, Maine, for six or seven years.

Eventually Ramsay settled in Kansas City for two years before moving to Louisville. While in Louisville he assisted in organizing the anti-tuberculosis movement, which became one of the most successful in the country. He was also a director of the state Children's Humane Society and worked successfully in other movements of "social betterment." The article goes on to relate that Rev. William Ramsay received an enthusiastic welcome at his installation service in Wellesley Hills that week.

At the 1909 annual meeting, the Standing Committee reports states, "It has been very gratifying to see so good an attendance at the church every Sunday and your committee hopes it will increase as pastor and people get better acquainted."

It appears that Rev. William Ramsay brought quite a different emphasis in his preaching and probably in his approach to people. Here is a short list of his early sermons in Wellesley Hills:

The Larger Mission of the Unitarian Churches

Poetry and the Higher Pantheism

The Religion of Jesus in Modern Life

The Uses of a Day

Liberal Religion in Literature

Jesus and the Buddha

The Religion of Jesus and the Individual

The early Unitarians were liberal Christians. They believed that Jesus was deeply informed by the Divine will if he was not God; therefore, the Bible was the basis of what they preached, and developing a better [Unitarian] understanding of that book was the burden of their preaching. A generation or two later, newly minted Unitarian ministers were looking at different expressions of God and other sources of religious inspiration—hence Ramsay's sermon topic "Poetry and the Higher Pantheism." They were also preaching on more humanistic topics that had direct application to their parishioners' daily lives, such as Ramsay's sermons "The Religion of Jesus in Modern Life" and "The Uses of a Day."

This change of sermon focus had begun to happen long before Albert Vorse and John Snyder came to Wellesley Hills, but William Ramsay brought a whole new religious world to the Wellesley Hills church. Undoubtedly some welcomed it as if they had been waiting for years for this transition to happen. Others were appalled.

At the Standing Committee meeting in January of 1910, the treasurer reported that they were about $1,000 behind where they needed to be in order to finish up the year in the black. By the end of the fiscal year in March, the treasury was in better shape. They voted to pay the pastor $2,000 for the coming year. They also voted to buy and install an electric motor to replace the hand-operated system of forcing air through the organ pipes.

In November the Standing Committee looked for a new worship service book and a new hymnal but failed to find anything they liked. Also in November, they discussed the matter of "looking after new members" and getting them to join. At first the matter was resolved by voting that people wishing to join should speak to the clerk of the Standing Committee. Later they decided to be a little more proactive and periodically circulate lists of the newcomers to people who might greet them. They became more successful at welcoming because new people were appearing with serious interest in joining in numbers not seen in recent years.

In February of 1911, the Standing Committee voted to grant the use of the church for a meeting led by Rabbi Fleischer—a noteworthy event because anti-Semitism was quite real in the suburbs of Boston at this time and for many, many years to come. They also voted that the parlor might be used for a women's suffrage meeting. Conservative they may have been in many ways, but their openness to the rights and dignity of other people may have distinguished them in the community.

The following month the Standing Committee voted that Mr. Ramsay and the music committee prepare a new order of service for the Standing Committee's perusal. The slight change they made was tried with what was reported as "good results." At another meeting, however, a motion to buy a new hymnal did not pass. These things take time, as people often get more attached to certain hymns than they do to their ministers.

At the annual meeting of 1911, the Standing Committee reported, "The year of the church has been one of progress. Under Mr. Ramsay's earnest ministry, the interest in and attendance at Sunday school has increased. The several organizations affiliated with the church have been active and prosperous." Elsewhere it was reported that the church school had fifty-two pupils and seven teachers. It was also reported that after years of debate and delay, an electric motor was finally installed, improving the sound of the organ considerably.

The often-pessimistic treasurer reported in January 1912 that a thirty percent increase in pledging would be necessary for the new year. At the same time new people were being voted into membership every month. It is interesting to note that in many New England Unitarian congregations, persons wanting to join were asked to declare their intentions to the governing board, and the board voted on whether or not they were perceived as having a good intent. The liberal religious commitment to make no requisite statement of commitment in order to join made it possible for outside groups with nefarious motives to become a voting majority in the congregation. One recent Unitarian minister noted how curious it was that all of the new members of his church or their spouses were members of the same benevolent order. A year after he had left for another parish, he came back and found the church closed and the building now used as a meeting hall for that same benevolent order.

In January of 1912, the Standing Committee asked Rev. William Ramsay to make a report to the annual meeting. It was a lengthy report, but parts of it clearly reflect the minister, his priorities, and even perhaps his soul:

> The routine work of the minister may seem monotonous and unromantic to those who have no experience of its pleasures, its often perplexing problems and its many surprises. The pastoral office of ministry is replete with opportunities for the highest kind of service that a man can render to his fellows.

> The minister is not infrequently brought into intimate relations of sympathy and possible helpfulness with men and women in times of mental and moral perplexity, of bereavement and sorrow, of doubt and questioning and of deep spiritual need. This is unquestionably the most valuable part of the minister's work—his most sacred office.

To many persons it has little or no significance because the circumstances of their own lives have not yet created any felt need of counsel, of consolation or of confession. But the time comes when such needs inevitably arise.

It would surprise such persons to find out how often the minister is called upon to render just such services. And for this he must keep himself prepared in mind and heart. This part of the minister's work does not lend itself to any formal report.

I have felt it to be my duty to call upon the members of the Society in their homes. This custom has been falling into disuse as the increasing miscellaneous demands upon the minister's time have become more exacting; and to many persons it is not regarded as at all important but to others—and especially to the aged and the infirm—it is often a source of pleasure and of comfort to receive this slight attention from their minister.

Ramsay goes on to explain the reasons for regular pulpit exchanges, which some parishioners resent and ministers crave. He describes the attendance at worship as "quite encouraging" but notes that supplementing the Sunday morning service with an afternoon vespers service has not had very encouraging results. He comments on the work of several affiliate groups of the church and then turns his attention to "Order and Form of Public Worship." He continues:

Our Unitarian congregations have been so long accustomed to the old Puritanical order of worship that any change or any liturgical innovation is apt to be uncongenial to many. And yet the entire trend of modern church worship has been in the direction of a larger use of the liturgical and musical elements and of a legitimate and beautiful symbolism. These elements of liturgy and symbolism and music appeal especially to the young; and it is well worth considering how far we can go toward meeting this need without falling into the rigidity of religious formalism.

In relation to social responsibility work at the church Ramsay wrote, "I am thoroughly convinced that the modern church cannot evade or escape from the responsibility or the imperious duty of seeking to understand and adjust itself and its attitude and its service to the pressing social needs of our time." He concludes, "Our Society is an item in the national asset of social righteousness, a distributing point of the Great Common Social Consciousness; and our individual relation to the church should mean a more vivid consciousness of social obligation and a deeper sense of social unity with all our fellows."

The social consciousness of the members of his congregation rarely left Wellesley Hills at this point. They were good at raising modest amounts of money for various groups of the identified needy, and they were moderately good at inviting speakers to the church to speak on the pressing problems of the day. Actual disciplined, on-the-scene involvement in the social issues of the day would take some time to materialize.

In June of 1912, it was reported that a Mr. Bartlett had arranged to give Mr. Ramsay an academic gown to wear in the pulpit on Sunday. Ramsay had migrated to the United States for a year at Harvard and then left for Louisville, Kentucky. Many Southern congregations not only did not require their ministers to robe, but some would have been troubled if they did. So Ramsay probably did not have a robe when he came to Wellesley where a pulpit gown was expected. It is amazing that it took the congregation well over a year before anyone thought to ask the minister why he was not wearing a robe and upon learning that he could not afford one, not figuring how to rectify the situation.

Looking forward to the coming year, the Sunday school reported that out of 180 members in the church nineteen lived out of town, 114 were not available for various reasons to teach, nineteen were flat out unwilling to serve, and fifteen had not yet been asked. In the meantime, several people who had taught this year were unable to continue teaching into the following year. Much seemed to depend on the role of the church school superintendent. In Wellesley Hills the superintendent was expected not only to administer the school but also to provide the worship experience and to provide whatever backup the teachers needed in the way of discipline.

When the superintendent was sufficiently commanding to preserve sanity in the classrooms, teachers often were reasonably happy with their experience. When classroom decorum suffered, the church school fell apart. The superintendent then usually quit the poorly paid job, and the job rebounded back to the minister who may or may not have been any good at it.

The 1913 annual meeting found Mr. Ramsay in a different mood. After an eloquent defense of his role as pastor in 1912, the following year he wrote:

> The pastoral duties connected with our church are not sufficient to tax the energies of a minister. I am convinced that the work of the minister and the religious efficiency of our church might be greatly enhanced by methods of mutual conference and of friendly criticism and counsel between the minister and the members of the Society. My convictions on this matter were strengthened by an informal conference held under the auspices of the Women's Alliance of our church, on the afternoon of February 25 in the church parlor when a most profitable discussion took place upon the work of our church and its opportunity to meet the religious needs of our growing community. The duty of our Society to make an aggressive effort to reach a large number of people not presently affiliated with any church organization was freely expressed by several of those present and valuable suggestions were offered.

Ramsay then goes on at length to point out that it does not take much to extend a warm welcome to strangers; it does take some recognition that something more than a curt nod or perfunctory handshake is required. He also laments, as others have before him, the lack of men in the Sunday morning congregations. This had been true of American Protestant congregations since the hold of Puritan religion waned.

The annual reports for this year show that the congregation is still growing strongly. Its affiliate organizations for men and women—the Unitarian Club for men and the Women's Alliance and Junior Alliance for women—were also growing and active. The year passed with nothing more than the usual issues arising while the community and the Society continued to grow.

In 1914 many of the nations of Europe went to war, but as far as can be determined from the local paper, the town of Wellesley was unfazed. Life went merrily along as it had with many no doubt convinced that war would not become an issue for them. President Woodrow Wilson had assured them of this. By 1917 there is a hint in the papers of concern at least for the Europeans who were suffering from the war.

Then in July of 1917, Rev. William Ramsay died. His obituary, written by one of his parishioners, covered three pages of the July 20, 1917, *Townsman*:

> He entered earnestly into the civic life of the town. Any movement of an uplifting or progressive character was heartily sure of his support and freest service. He was greatly interested in the Wellesley forum because it dealt with a wide range of important subjects from the standpoint of experience as well as theory. His democratic attitude led to the formation of strong friendships with all classes of people. . . .
>
> To interpret the spiritual viewpoint of a man whose vision transcended the formal and conventional conceptions of religion is a difficult if not impossible task. The fundamental idea of religion as the bond between man and the Infinite Life is so vast that it may

easily lend itself to the formation of creeds and dogmas. With these Mr. Ramsey had little sympathy. It is impossible to state genuine religious thought and feeling in cold, formal creedal or dogmatic terms. Mr. Ramsay, even though preaching from the pulpit of a liberal church, strongly felt this limitation, hence his greatest effort was to the presentation of religion in its larger, its more universal aspects. He felt that "religion is life, an attitude of the mind, a thing of the heart and the will which is good. [Man] lives for his efforts for higher things. This eternal pursuit of the ideal with its many tortures and its many glorious joys—this is life. . . .

The steadfastness of his faith was well manifested in the calmness, the serenity even, with which he approached the gateway to another and probably a larger aspect of life: the gateway which we call death. His last message to the world was one of good cheer, of readiness to meet the issues of the new journey with absolute trust in the outcome; with complete confidence in the Guide.

Marion Niles, who was very active in the church throughout her life, wrote, "Mr. Ramsay was of a gentle and sensitive nature, one to whom it was easy to speak in times of concern or trouble. As I remember, his sermons sent me home inspired and thoughtful."

CHAPTER 8

Through War and Epidemic

THE MINISTER WHO succeeded Rev. William Ramsay in the Wellesley Hills Unitarian church actually began his career as a Baptist minister. Charles Potter's family were active members in the Baptist church of Marlboro, Massachusetts, the town where Potter was born in 1885. As a young man, Potter obtained a license to preach. In 1907 he enrolled in Bucknell University, transferred to Brown and then could not afford it, and went back to Bucknell. While at Brown he was introduced to liberal German theology which began to create some doubts in his mind about his Baptist faith.

Upon graduation from Bucknell, Potter enrolled in Newton Theological Seminary, now called Andover Newton, and graduated in 1913 with a Bachelor of Divinity degree. While serving his first parish in Edmonton, Alberta, Canada, he became interested in the preaching of the Reverend John Dietrich in Spokane, Washington. Dietrich was one of the first humanist ministers in the American Unitarian Association. Though still a Baptist, Potter found himself intrigued by this human-centered rather than God-centered approach to religion. He left the Baptist church and was called to the Unitarian church in his hometown of Marlboro, Massachusetts.

Potter stayed in Marlboro for almost two years. When he arrived he had vigorously negotiated a contract in which he promised to meet several growth objectives for the church. If he did so, he would receive a sizeable increase in compensation. He met those objectives. The annual meeting came and went, and nothing was said about changing the minister's compensation. The board of trustees was completely unprepared for a negotiating minister and probably forgot the clauses he had insisted be in his contract. When he expressed his dissatisfaction to the congregation at large, they said, "Well that can be easily remedied. We'll call another annual meeting and grant you your increase."

Potter said, "It's too late. Out of several offers I have had recently I have chosen the Wellesley Hills Unitarian Church at a salary of $3,000 a year plus parsonage. My letter of acceptance was read there this morning. And there is a provision . . . whereby the salary is increased to $3,500 at the end of a year if my services are satisfactory." This would mark the first increase of a Wellesley Hills minister's salary since 1871.

In his autobiography *The Preacher and I,* Potter notes that members of the Marlboro church's board of trustees attended his installation service in Wellesley Hills and button-holed every member of the Wellesley board to tell them the circumstances of his leaving Marlboro and warning them not to make the same mistakes. Apparently they did not listen. Potter remembers his first days in Wellesley:

> One of the many interesting persons we met in our new parish was a lively woman of eighty, Mrs. Theoda J. Hill, wealthy widow and daughter of a railroad man.
>
> She arrived with her paid companion at the parsonage as soon as we had the furniture unpacked and arranged, and immediately said to my wife, 'That sofa shouldn't be over there. It belongs here,

and that chair should be in this corner. Oh dear, we never have the furniture arranged this way in the parsonage!"

Mrs. [Clara] Potter walked right up to the domineering little old lady, looked her straight in the eye, and said, "This is the parsonage true enough; but while I am living in it, it is my home, and I shall arrange the furniture exactly as I please."

I was aghast at my wife's temerity, for peace in the parish seemed to me more important than the arrangement of furniture; but to my surprise and relief, Mrs. Hill actually embraced Mrs. Potter and exclaimed, "My dear child, I've been waiting forty years to find a minister's wife with spunk. You're quite right about the furniture of course. You and I will get along famously. I hear you have three active little boys. I'll darn their socks every week." And she did.

Remembering the highlights of his brief stay in Wellesley Hills, Potter mentioned the day of the armistice, November 11, 1918. He rushed across the street from the parsonage to the church and "rang the bell with such vigor and for such a long time that I was mildly reproved therefore."

Also memorable was the flu epidemic that began a few weeks before the armistice. Potter wrote, "Many of the church people worked in the temporary hospital which was set up at the Maugus Club, and I went into the homeopathic hospital and served as an orderly and general assistant. When it was discovered that I was a clergyman, I was assigned the duty of informing the dying of their approaching death

Rev. Charles Frances Potter

and asking if they had any messages for their relatives. None of them would believe it however."

During this time the Protestant congregations in Wellesley closed their doors for about a month so as not to contribute to the spread of the disease. Potter put this sentence on the outside bulletin board, "Church closed. Ignoring disease never was and never will be good religion." He was quoted in the local newspaper as saying, "If you could hear what the overworked nurses and doctors in various hospitals are saying about clergymen who persist in herding their followers together in defiance of the laws of health during this epidemic, you would realize the truth of the sentence on our church bulletin."

One of the highlights of Potter's ministry was successfully maneuvering a different person into the role of treasurer. At the subsequent annual meeting, parishioners did not hear the usual gloom and doom that had characterized treasurers' reports for years. Instead, they learned that the Society had a surplus of $4,000.

Wellesley College had traditionally been standoffish and disapproving of the Unitarian Church. But Katherine Lee Bates, author of "American the Beautiful" and head of the English Literature Department, and her companion had a daughter in the Unitarian Sunday school. While making a pastoral call, Potter met Bates and came to admire her greatly. She obtained an invitation for Potter to speak at the Wellesley College Chapel. She told him he had better do his best because he was only the second Unitarian ever to be asked to speak there, and the first had not been well received.

Eventually Wellesley College students started attending the Unitarian church and continued during Potter's ministry. Also attending from time to time was Roger Babson who everyone knew was a member of the Hills Congregational Church. The minister at the Hills church told Potter not to get too swelled a head about Babson's presence. Roger attended the opening of the Hills church service every Sunday. If he thought he knew where the sermon was going he slipped over to the Unitarians to see if Potter had stories or ideas that were any different.

According to a review in the *Wellesley Townsman*, Potter made the following argument in his first sermon in Wellesley Hills, titled "The God Likeness of Service":

> Mr. Potter pointed out at once the seeming contradiction of ideas and argued for a new conception of God more consonant with this new age where service rather than royalty is the great word. He showed that nature revealed God is the servant helper of men "who made the flames fire his tools, sweeps the cities with his winds and bursts forth increasingly in the varied energy which we call life. The Bible also manifests God as the Great Helper for it begins with him at work making worlds, and it ends with him wiping tears from the eyes of sufferers. . . . Humanity itself points to the God likeness of service, for all the highest personalities have been the greatest workers of the world."

Jesus, he later points out, was "the embodiment of love at work." Some of Potter's early sermon topics include:

The Training of Desire: A Study in Scientific Character Building

Loyalty

The Clumsy King

Who is the Liberal?

The Price of Possession

The Education of Conscience

The Authority of Conscience

The Ruling Passion: A Study in the Psychology of Human Conduct

Unlike John Snyder or even William Ramsay, Charles Potter was very much taken with new knowledge and new theories, which he seemed to accept as true and wanted his congregation to know that they had all better get with the advance of science. One wonders if, at age thirty-four, he was not a little hard on his parishioners, continually asking them to move along with him, leaving comfortable faith affirmations behind.

At the annual meeting of 1919, the Standing Committee comments, "The year just passed has been one of substantial interest and progress in the affairs of the Society. While it might be marked in a dozen ways, the best visual evidence of interest and progress is in the increased size of the congregation at the Sunday morning service." It continued, "A church must go forward or backward. It cannot stand still. Ours is now well in the forward move and should be kept in this condition by the generous financial support of its parishioners." This same report goes on to remind the congregation that it entered into a one-year contract with Potter with the option that it could be renewed as an indefinite period contract at a vote of that meeting.

In his report, Potter seems to reflect on his reorganization of the Sunday school. It was not all he could have wished, but a start had been made in a "program of reconstruction." The church school was brought into closer touch with the service of worship. The minister and the Standing Committee—mostly the minister—were placed in charge of religious education rather than lay leaders as had been the case. The courses have been thought out and systematized, and the minister now runs a "normal school for teachers" so that everyone feels they are progressing in the same direction.

Potter relates that he made 225 calls, preached forty sermons, and gave twenty-two lectures to the Wellesley School of Religious Education, which may have been shared with some of the other liberal Protestant churches. Written examinations were conducted from time to time, reflecting how seriously this minister took this work and that he wanted parents to expect the children to do well on these exams.

On April 30, 1919, a special meeting of the congregation was called. It was explained that their agreement with Mr. Potter had been that if all went well between minister and congregation, the minister would be voted indefinite tenure at the salary of $3,000.

Potter's memory of this incident is that the church originally promised him $3,500 at the next annual meeting if all had gone well. In any event, nothing had been done about a salary increase at the annual meeting, and it took them a while to rectify the mistake at the special meeting. By the time they did, it was too late as far as Potter was concerned. His parishioners read in the newspaper that he had accepted a call to the West Side Church in New York City. He stayed there for six years.

Eventually Potter did some fundraising for Antioch College. Later on he became a spokesman for humanism and founded a humanist church in New York City. During the Scopes Trial he served as consultant on Biblical matters to Clarence Darrow and became a widely known lecturer and debater on the national religious scene.

Of the three men who served the Wellesley Hills Unitarian Society before Potter, two had died in office after long ministries and the third probably would have preferred to stay but was persuaded to move on. So the church may not have been fully prepared for a minister who probably from the beginning had set his eyes on a career elsewhere. It would not be the last time.

CHAPTER 9

The Twenties Arrive

SIDNEY AHLSTROM, A leading historian of American religion, had this to say about the 1920s:

> The decade of the twenties is the most sharply defined decades in American history. Marked off by the war at one end and the Depression at the other it has a character of its own—ten restless years roaring from jubilation to despair amid international and domestic dislocation. . . . Religiously oriented critics of all parties have usually spoken of these ten years as a tragic display of obscurantism, superficiality, complacency and futile conflict. What has been lost to mind is the fact that the twenties were an exciting time of social transformation, intellectual resolution and artistic triumph.

Our rather limited ground view of Wellesley in the 1920s is a little cheerier and justifiably so, since Wellesley at this time blossomed and grew. Local historian Elizabeth Hinchcliffe writes:

> And so began what looked like a decade of partying. New stores sprang up throughout town, and they featured clothes, makeup and jewelry for "flappers." Dancing at the Maugus Club had never been so popular nor had football games and raccoon coats. . . .

Nearly everyone had a car now, as fathers and sons taught each other how to drive. Cars were the center of people's lives—loved, photographed and protected against the elements. Family excursions had a new game—counting the number of flat tires on the way home and hoping you didn't get one yourself. . . .

By the end of the decade there were more than 50 clubs and organizations in Wellesley ranging from the new Boy Rangers to the American Legion and the Wellesley Historical Society. This most notable characteristic of the social activities of this decade was that the more time and money people had, the more they seemed encouraged to put it to good causes.

There would, perhaps, be no better time for Wellesley than the twenties. It was the era of the conscious development of the town. The raw materials were there, the ideas had been introduced, and now the leaders and developers were concentrating on shaping a perfect town. Homes were built, elegant lovely ones with manicured yards. . . .

During this decade Wellesley chose to become a suburb, a well mannered, well maintained residential community. To some it meant security in a certain way of life; to others it meant exclusiveness. The most heated exchange of letters in the *Townsman* was about the reported new "snobbishness in the town."

Growth such as this usually means that the religious institutions in town will grow as well, and in Wellesley they did. The Unitarian Society grew to the point at which there were 250 children in the church school, fifty of whom were under the age of five. They needed the right minister to fuel this growth, and it turns out they found him.

The Reverend Walter Samuel Swisher was offered the position about five months after the departure of Charles Potter. Swisher was born in Meadville, Pennsylvania. While still a young man, he became secretary to one of the chief executives of the Westinghouse Machine

Company and organist to one of the largest churches in Pittsburgh. In 1906 he entered Meadville Theological School and graduated in 1910. He studied for a year in Germany and then served the Unitarian congregation in Passaic, New Jersey. In 1914 he was called to All Souls Church in New London, Connecticut. Reading between the lines, we gather that Swisher was a young man when he came to Wellesley Hills and that he was married. We also learn that he was already a proficient organist and authority of church music. In 1927 he

Rev. Walter Samuel Swisher

wrote a book titled *Psychology for the Music Teacher* and later another book titled *Religion and the New Psychology*. Among Swisher's first sermons were the following topics:

Modern Literary Movements and their Relations to Modern Times

The Opportunity for the Liberal Faith

The Still Small Voice: The Search for God in the Soul

Beside the Still Waters: Psalm 23

The Divinity of Daily Life

The Filibuster

Ye Must Be Born Again

The Things Men Need, a sermon series with sermons titled:
Appreciation, Work, Love, Worship, Play

The 1920s marked the beginning of a time when ministers and social workers were fascinated with the thought of modern psychologists and believed that if men and women were aware of this new context in which to view one's own lives, they would live with less conflict and self doubt. In contrast to his immediate predecessor Potter, Swisher seemed to have been less concerned with transforming human institutions and more devoted to leading individual souls to greater happiness.

Whatever was happening at the Unitarian Society during the early years of Swisher's stewardship was working. Shortly after he arrived, the *Wellesley Townsman* commented on the fact that the turnout for a turkey dinner sponsored by the layman's league and had been planned for the parish house—at that time a rented house at the corner of Washington Street and Eton Court—had to be moved to the Maugus Club because of its numbers. The paper quipped, "When church gatherings grow so large that their own parish house accommodations no longer accommodate we begin to open our eyes and ask, 'What is going on in this new day?' and inquire whether the church is not having a new awakening. . . . As a furniture house of New York and Pittsburgh used to say, 'Watch us grow!'"

While we do not have manuscripts of Swisher's early sermons, we do have sermon squibs and teasers that give more than a hint of what he believed:

> *Is There a Decline in Religious Feeling, and If So Why?*
>
> *Are We Looking After Our Young People As We Ought?*
>
> *The Changing Basis of Liberal Religion: S.D. Gordon, the evangelist states that if a man finds Christ all else will follow. Will it? Do we not need intelligence in our religious life as well as poetry?*
>
> *The Old Testament in Light of Modern Psychology*
>
> *Castles in Spain*
>
> *How We Live with Self-Created Issues*
>
> *The Road to Tomorrow: The road to tomorrow stretches with its wonderful promise of bright and better things to come and its hopes and*

its fears, its joys and its sorrow. To go forward with shining faces, ready for the new day, is a test of our courage and character.

The Quest for Happiness: Why do we fail to find happiness? Because we carry our own problems with us. Happiness comes through unselfishness and service. The self-seeking man is never happy.

The Way Out: Plunged with an after-war chaos we are still seeking "the way out."

What is Truth? Is it something hard and fixed for all time? Or is it a dynamic something that grows with human evolution?

In the later part of 1921, the members of the Society celebrated the fiftieth anniversary of their incorporation in a worship service plus post-service reminiscences. New England Unitarian Universalists who now join congregations that are already centuries old rarely have the opportunity to look back on the struggles of their fledgling congregation to survive and finally to succeed. The members of the Unitarian Society of Wellesley Hills had just that chance. At the anniversary celebration, Isaac Sprague chaired the meeting that featured remarks by Louis Cornish, the general secretary of the American Unitarian Association; Henry Winton, one of its oldest members; and Walter Swisher, though we have no copy of his remarks.

Going back over the pride he and his contemporaries had always taken over the resilience of their church, Winton spoke of several people who typified that early spirit. Alvin Fuller was one of the pioneers who could always be found at every event of the church. He served the community as postmaster and railroad agent, and he usually distributed the mail from his hat as he came into church Sunday morning. John W. Shaw was another whose heart and soul were interested in the church. Winton remarked, "I have seen him walking by the church and hesitate, stop and turn, look with an air of pride and then go on with a pleased expression."

Winton continues, "The life of the church in those [earliest] days was full of activity. A course of lectures together with coffee parties through the winter months and a two- or three-day fair usually held in a tent on the lawn beside the chapel, and a midsummer picnic were always events in which the whole community were interested, and all of these affairs augmented the church finances."

He went on to mention Albert Vorse's wonderful ministry and the fact that his wife was still alive and present with them that night. He recognized that subsequent ministries—Snyder, Ramsay and Potter—had been brief by comparison, and then he spoke of Swisher. "We now have with us one whom you have all learned to know. I name him 'Youth.' We bespeak for him a prosperous and happy ministry," Winton concluded.

As Wellesley historian Hinchcliffe mentioned, automobiles fascinated people at this time. Of course people were interested when the new Unitarian minister purchased an Overland Red Bird automobile. It made the *Townsman*. An advertisement for this car shows a red four-or-five-passenger touring car. The text describes it: "Fine feathers make fine birds finer. The big new Overland Red Bird has a more powerful engine, longer wheelbase, roomier body, rich Mandalay maroon finish, khaki top, nickel trimmings, Fisk cord tires, bumpers front and rear. The most automobile in the world for the money. $795." The ad implies that this car is certainly a youthful statement for the new Unitarian minister.

As we follow the growth of the church over the next few years, we find activities that must have required a great deal of energy and effort. The young people's group—sometimes called "The Fraternity" or "Y.P.R.U"—had frequent vesper services with guest speakers, organ accompaniment for hymns, and sometimes choristers. These vespers were strongly enabled by the church staff and other adults, and the speakers frequently came out from the American Unitarian

Association. We know this was the 1920s—and not the 1960s—because if these young folks were going to do worship, they were going to do it in a way both they and the adults could approve.

Other activities at this time included frequent church suppers, one of which was labeled "an old fashioned country supper." The Laymen's League—an organization of churchmen—frequently invited well-known speakers out to address them. One notable speaker, Florence Beck of the American Unitarian Association, gave a presentation on how their new curriculum used the Bible in an age appropriate way. The Alliance—an organization of churchwomen—met regularly and invited well-known speakers to address them. They also constituted a large "kitchen cabinet" on the state of the church and its finances.

Every November the church held an annual harvest meal that also involved the preparation of overflowing baskets of food for the less fortunate. One year the Society's annual fair had the theme of a gypsy encampment with the women dressed accordingly. There was also at least one vaudeville show, which they called "The Unitarian Follies." In addition, the coach of a Harvard team came out to talk with the church school about what had inspired him.

There were also a few events at Wellesley College, which now had a Unitarian Club. The Layman's League formed a "motor corps" to deliver shut-ins to church. The activities list goes on. A contemporary Unitarian Universalist might note the absence of what we call "social action." The Wellesley Unitarians of the 1920s would not have recognized the term. They did do social service in the form of collecting money or goods to give generously to agencies that would handle the distribution. If someone had suggested political action to right some injustices or change the conditions that left people poor, they would have suggested this was inappropriate or divisive or perhaps even socialistic, which had very negative connotations back then.

Since Swisher probably wrote most of the publicity squibs for the newspaper, we learn that he was a busy fellow, much called upon as a guest preacher and lecturer. In March of 1922, he was the featured attraction of a Laymen's League meeting in Memphis, played an organ concert featuring some of his own compositions, and then preached at the building site of their new church.

In June, Swisher told the Free Religious Association, "The church as presently organized was more concerned with providing a refuge for fear-stricken souls than in diffusing the light of progress." He added, "If the church failed to keep pace with the onward march, it would inevitably degenerate until at length it would become a refuge for the neurotic, the supine and the unfit." He added, "The most helpful phase in sight was the new humanism in philosophy and religion."

This was a strange speech for the minister of a comfortable suburban parish whose members were still quite committed to the Biblical tradition, if not to Biblical theology. It appears to mark a turn in the direction of this minister's thinking, perhaps even some disillusionment with his present congregation. But it would not be the last turn in his thinking.

Judging from Swisher's speaking engagements, he was one of the leading Unitarian interpreters of the philosophies of Freud and Dewey. He gave frequent lectures throughout the Boston area and beyond on this new thought and what he felt it meant. But over the course of the next several years what he actually preached to his home congregation became more conservative. In his 1925 sermon "The Covert from the Storm," he said, "This post war world is a world of chaotic impulses and a breaking up of old things. Only as we rely upon God the rock of ages can we find covert from the storm and peace from the conflict. To the soul that trusts him, God is a strong salvation." [The word "covert" is a now an old-fashioned word meaning "cover."] This is a bit removed from the minister who two years earlier spoke somewhat contemptuously of "fear-stricken souls" and envisioned the march of the brave, armored by truth, into the future.

A March 1924 article in the local paper reported that the Unitarian church had experienced "100% growth in 4 years" with a Sunday school enrollment of nearly 250 children. They are considering building a new church building to replace the present one, the article continued. A twenty-one-member committee has been meeting and proposed a building that could possibly be situated at the end of Grantland Road [possibly opposite the current Hills Congregational Church]. It would be of "Georgian character with red brick." The parsonage would comprise one wing of the church, and on the opposite side would be the parish hall. This would mean that the church could sell both the parsonage they owned and the parish house, the proceeds from which would help to finance this building.

Since church records for this period cannot be found, it is hard to figure out what happened to this proposal. In August the minister announced that extensive renovations have been made to the church they have. "When all this is finished," he wrote, "we will have a lovely little Medieval chapel. All the woodwork—ceilings, trusses, wainscoting and pews—have been refurbished in a walnut brown. The walls are an Italian putty color from a sample brought from Italy. The pew ends have been reshaped in a gothic style." So what happened to the new vision of the Georgian colonial church proposed by a twenty-one-member committee? We do not yet know.

A fire broke out in the sanctuary at 6:40 p.m. on Saturday, September 19, 1924. A short in a light switch caused extensive damage to the interior of the sanctuary. A newspaper article reports, "The fire proved a costly one. The rear of the church was badly burned as well as the roof above, scorched. Water contributed to the loss doing heavy damage to the organ as well as warping the newly laid cork floor and discoloring the pews. Also the heat cracked the beautiful colored glass window above the pulpit." The damaged glass window was not the rose-colored window that now has prominence in the sanctuary, but a predecessor.

In three or four months the sanctuary was repaired, but the organ could not be. Fortunately, the church became the beneficiary of a gift from Mrs. Louville Niles: a Hook & Hastings three-manual organ drawn to the specifications of the Reverend Swisher, an accomplished organist himself. Because the sanctuary was not large, the organ was "voiced for beauty and variety of tone rather than power although the great organ will have ample power to carry congregational singing. It will be the last word in artistic voicing." For several years that followed, the organ was frequently requested for area recitals.

On Easter Sunday of the following year, the sanctuary was packed and celebrated the welcoming of eighty new members in the last four years.

CHAPTER 10

The Economic Bubble Bursts

THE WELLESLEY UNITARIANS held their traditional flower Sunday on June 25, 1925. When I inherited this tradition in 1977, I assumed it had been established in the 1940s as a response to Norbert Capek's "Flower Service" in Prague, Czechoslovakia, and his martyrdom at the hands of the Nazis. For twenty-three years no one ever told me differently; however, it turns out that the Unitarian Society of Wellesley Hills has been celebrating a flower Sunday since they began around 1871. It may even have been the creation of Albert Buel Vorse.

As the weeks and months of 1925 passed by, the church continued to prosper and grow. The Reverend Swisher seemed to be offering a continuous series of lectures on topics of psychology, religion, and philosophy, and they were well attended. Because of the high quality of the new organ, the church also sponsored a number of concerts and recitals. The youth group continued to churn out great activities and programs.

In October of 1925, representatives from all religious denominations in Wellesley were invited to gather monthly for the Interchurch Committee of Wellesley. Its stated purpose was "a strong desire on the part of the people of the different congregations to work together on such questions as the vital importance of religion in the life of the individual and the community, the need of a finer type of home life, and the necessity for a more thorough-going moral and religious training if young people are to be properly equipped for their life work."

Obviously these broad purposes could not be achieved only by offering monthly meetings highlighting distinguished lecturers, but that is what they did. Every age has its own way of coping with the fact that its children are choosing their own routes to the future. Turning out to hear experts in the new psychologies was the vastly more favored way in the 1920s. We should applaud those parents who cared enough about their children to show up, and many did.

In the spring of 1927, members of the Standing Committee began to consider whether or not to build a parish house connected to the church. The need had been partially filled by buying a house across the street, but the church had grown much too large for that house to suffice. When this concern was first presented at the annual meeting, it was coupled with a proposal by an architectural firm that did not employ any local architects. This proposal was voted down with some heat because no one knew the recommended architects. That committee was replaced. The Standing Committee was encouraged to keep on working the idea.

A second proposal reworked the basement of the church to provide the extra space needed, and the Standing Committee voted this down. Fundraising this year was about $1,000 below where it should have been, and no one was feeling that they were "in the money."

A third proposal involved using the Livermore House—right next to the church and owned by the Society—as a temporary parish house and church school until such time as the parish felt able to afford a new parish house.

Finally on February 26, 1929, the congregation voted to construct a parish hall, to raise $50,000 for it, and to borrow the rest from the American Unitarian Association and a bank. Then on October 29, 1929, the stock market crashed. In December of 1929, the parish met again to assess how things were going. They learned that building pledges were about $3,000 ahead of where they might have been expected to be, but pledges to the annual budget were down. The die was cast, however, and they pushed on.

New Parish Hall addition to church

A *Wellesley Townsman* article described plans for the new wing in glowing terms:

> The new building is in complete accord with the church to which it is joined by a tower of Norman design, built of fieldstone. The fields and quarries hereabouts furnish a great variety of rough granite suitable for stonewalls and buildings.

The building is thirty feet wide and ninety-two feet long and is designed to conform to the lines of the church. Full advantage has been taken of the site so that very little of the lower floor will be below ground. The lower floor with its classrooms, dining hall, parlor, serving room and kitchen will have adequate lighting and air from the large windows.

The large assembly hall will be paneled in pine, lightly stained to give it the appearance of age. The lighting fixtures hung from the truss and designed by Mr. William Roger Greeley, the architect, are in the form of Old English wrought brass lanterns. They will be executed at the forge of Proctor Academy. The style of the hall with its scissors trusses is Old English, the architect finding the inspiration for the roof from a twelfth-century English castle hall. At the end of the hall will be an ample stage with large proscenium, suitable for plays and pageants.

The article goes on to state, "This new building will not only provide adequate, commodious and beautiful quarters for the Unitarian Society of Wellesley Hills and all of its organizations, but the minister and the people will delight to extend the courtesy of its use to the other churches and organizations of our community. We trust that it will be a center of religious and social activities." The article does not note that the small round room at the top of the tower was designated the minister's office. When or if it was used that way remains to be seen.

On Easter of 1929 a new rose window was unveiled. The earlier fire had cracked the window that was in the center of the old sanctuary; this new rose window replaces it. The new rose window was given by Mrs. Charles Warren Hatch and executed by Earl Edward Sanborn. According to a *Wellesley Townsman* article:

The outer circle consists of twelve panels enclosing in a small circle one of the signs of the Zodiac. This outer circle may be termed "The Wheel of Time." The central trefoil bears two human figures, one prone upon the ground, the other rising above him with arm stretched upward. Above the erect figure is a star toward which he reaches. The significance of the window as a whole is man rising through time above his baser material self to a nobler spiritual plane of being; in other words it is "The Progress of Man Onward and Upward Forever." The figures are not intended to be conspicuous or pictorial; they are an integral part of the design.

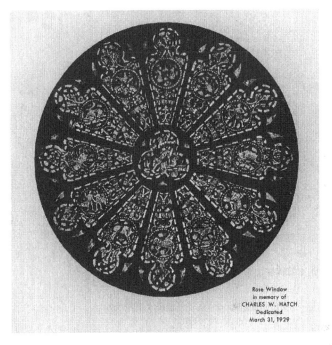

Rose Window
in memory of
CHARLES W. HATCH
Dedicated
March 31, 1929

The window is done in the rich colors of thirteenth-century glass: crimson, the symbol of divine love; blue, denoting constancy and truth; yellow, the symbol of the goodness of God; green, the vernal color signifying victory and the hope of immortality; violet, symbolizing victory through suffering. The background of the small circles is Canterbury blue—blue with a slightly greenish tone. Crimson is the prevailing color of the window.

The general design of the window is like that of the English rose window and somewhat like the rose window in the Cathedral of Soissons in France. These windows are called "rose windows" because their panels resemble the open petals of a flower. "In a rose window," says Mr. Sanborn, "design and color are the important thing; the figures must be a part of the design.

In hindsight we know that America was entering a dark time in its economic history that would last up to the start of World War II. After October of 1929, the minister and members knew that the stock market was volatile, but perhaps they hoped it would right itself and there would be course corrections.

In 1929 and 1930, there was very little in the *Wellesley Townsman* suggesting the people of Wellesley knew that their lives were about to change dramatically and not in pleasant ways. Among the articles about the Unitarian church that appeared were:

> A group of laymen were meeting to discuss "religious issues" with the Reverend Swisher, and "great interest is shown in these meetings."

> Twenty new members join the congregation.

> A group formed to write, produce, and direct plays to be held in the new parish hall, which seems to have been built precisely for that purpose.

> The Easter service was packed, as other major services had been all year.

On Walter Swisher's tenth anniversary with the church, the congregation surprised him and his wife with a celebration and a gift of money with the instruction that they spend it on travel. In thanking them, Swisher said, "The last ten years had taught him that fewer things are essential in successful living, that these years had given him broader tolerance and deeper sympathies, that they have increased his interest in people and have brought him a deeper faith." He and his wife sailed for Bermuda on May 10, and the vice president of the American Unitarian Association occupied his pulpit until June.

In February of 1930, the Unitarian Society hosted a "Preaching Mission," sponsored by the denomination's Layman's League. It consisted of seven evening addresses and one Sunday morning service from February 16 to February 23 on the topic of "The Imperative Need for Religion in Our Modern World." The preacher was Frederick May Eliot, minster of the Unity Church in St. Paul, Minnesota. Eliot was highly respected in the American Unitarian Association and eventually became its president. Each evening service was accompanied by music "of a high order" and songs from area choirs. According to a later article in the *Townsman*, the services were well attended and successful, although what they were looking for in the way of success was never clear.

During Lent in 1930, the Unitarian church and the Hills Congregational church held combined Easter week services. The ministers of the two churches alternated preaching and conducting the service every other day until Easter Sunday when each congregation worshipped separately. This had been going on for several years and would continue for several more years. At the end of the church year, the two congregations would join together in a walk up Maugus Hill for a picnic and a joint service conducted by one minister or the other alternately. Maugus Hill was still unsettled at this time.

Historically the Hills congregation and the Unitarian congregation had been close since 1871 when Albert Vorse and the Hills minister worked to make it so. At various times each congregation had had to leave its sanctuary—usually to allow repairs to the building—and accepted the offer of the other to hold joint services conducted alternately by the two pastors. It is remarkable that this relationship continued for almost sixty years, reflecting perhaps that many members of each congregation were less concerned with doctrinal differences and more concerned with neighborliness and fellowship. Many years later when the Congregational churches merged with the Evangelical and Reformed denomination, moving further to the right of the religious spectrum, and the Unitarian congregations moved left, many of them quite explicitly out of the Christian family, the relationship between the two Wellesley congregations changed and will probably not change back.

In July of 1930, the *Wellesley Townsman* began to recognize in its articles that the depression was going to hang around for a while. The first evidence was the announcement of a weekly column offering to help people who were willing to identify themselves as looking for work.

At the same time Walter Swisher's sermons began to take on a more pastoral tone, perhaps recognizing that the wisdom we look for was perhaps not so clearly found by brushing up on the latest insights of science or psychology. He also leaned more directly than he had earlier on God as a source of strength in difficult times. Following are some of his sermon titles:

Still Waters

Rocky Steps

The Fullness of Life: How is Happiness Measured

Faith in an Age of Doubt

Must We Have Certitude?

The Beauty of Imperfection

Compensations

God Our Strength, the first of five sermons

Toward the Light

Then came the matter of Mrs. Dove. Mrs. Dove had been superintendent of the church school for many years, and the school had grown considerably. Many were happy with her leadership and gave little thought to how things were actually run. It is possible that Mrs. Dove had begun to think about the church school as her own little world of which she was benevolent boss. It is also possible that members of church school committees over the years had begun to feel the same way.

A time came, however, when some parents began to feel differently. They got the ear of the church school committee and began to air these concerns at meetings about which Mrs. Dove was not informed nor invited. When she found out, she became incensed and sent out a letter to most of the congregation expressing her grievances and her decision to resign. The Standing Committee learned about this letter with everyone else.

When asked about her grievances and why she had not been more forthcoming to the Standing Committee before sending a letter of resignation to the parish, Mrs. Dove explained that she did not see herself as accountable to the Standing Committee or to the church school committee but to the parish, which she believed had hired her. Following is a summary of Mrs. Dove's grievances from the Standing Committee minutes:

> The church school committee had held a meeting to which she had not been invited.

> They had, at that meeting, appointed a treasurer to take charge of the church school finances, which previously Mrs. Dove had handled.

> At that meeting the church school committee compiled a list of instructions that they sent to her, asking that she follow them.

The church school committee was functioning in a supervisory capacity which they had no right to do.

In attempting to understand Mrs. Dove's grievances, the Standing Committee summarized them as follows:

Mrs. Dove believes she was hired and is only responsible to the parish.

She is, in fact, accountable to the Standing Committee, the church school committee, and the minister all of whom act in a supervisory capacity where she is concerned.

The Standing Committee would like the church's relationship to Mrs. Dove to continue with those understandings.

The Standing Committee asked her to withdraw her resignation, which she declined to do. It seemed necessary to accept her resignation along with the committee's regret and appreciation for her years of valuable service. However, since Mrs. Dove's letter, which everyone had received, challenged the very nature of the way the church is governed, they also found it necessary to send a letter of their own to the congregation, and they did so. In the meantime, Mrs. Dove had accepted an offer from Framingham.

Misunderstandings like this are fairly typical in many congregations. They waste time and energy and inevitably create hurt feelings that linger long after the disagreement has been resolved or put aside. Sometimes the supervision of one or more lay leaders has been so aggressive and so manifestly unfair that long-term harm is done to the congregation. Sometimes the employee has entertained the idea that nothing he/she does is out of line or, as in the case of Mrs. Dove, that he/she is employed by the parish and is not responsible to the specific lay leaders who have been elected to govern. The history of this disagreement suggests that every full- or half-time church employee should receive a written contract that, among other things, spells out to whom they are accountable and how their performance may be evaluated.

No matter what happens, scuffles like this one almost always reflect on the minister. It may be that the minister had nothing to do with the conflict, but many members of the congregation will assume that a good minister would have been able to do something to avoid it. At worst, those who may have already been a bit dissatisfied with the minister will come forth and proclaim that he/she must have had some part in this employee's dissatisfaction. The long-term consequences of such barely suppressed rumbling can be imagined. Since Mrs. Dove briefly mentioned her unhappiness with Swisher, long-term consequences may have been set in motion.

On June 4, 1933, the congregation accepted the resignation of Walter Samuel Swisher with deep regret. The leadership might have had a clue as to what was going on because Swisher had been unable to attend the annual meeting for that year. He was committed to preach at the Church of the Messiah in St. Louis to which he was subsequently called. As the article in the *Wellesley Townsman* explained, "The Church of the Messiah is one of the oldest churches in the city and has had a line of distinguished ministers. It has had an important place in the development of the academic and cultural life of St. Louis." The article continues:

> When asked how he felt about leaving Wellesley, Mr. Swisher replied, "More than half of the total years of my ministry have been spent in Wellesley Hills. The people of both church and community have been uniformly kind and friendly. I regret that I must leave the many friends who have given me so many expressions of affection."
>
> Many changes have taken place in the Unitarian Church and in the town of Wellesley since Mr. Swisher came in 1920. "I feel," said Mr. Swisher, "that the work I came to do has been accomplished. The church is now a thriving, well-organized and active church.

My whole effort has been directed to building up a strong organization as well as drawing a congregation to hear my preaching. I have small patience with those ministers who are interested only in drawing large congregations and have not the interest of the church at heart."

Walter Swisher deserved all of the praise he got for his thirteen years in Wellesley. Presiding in the time of considerable growth, his church admitted more members than there were in Wellesley at the time the church was founded. He left to serve one of the major Unitarian Christian congregations in the country as well as a congregation and a city that would have treasured his intellectual leadership. He had been moving in this direction anyway. We will never know how much the dispute with Mrs. Dove had affected the way in which he was now received, but the congregation's leadership gave him a heartfelt thank you and farewell.

CHAPTER 11

The Minister as Scholar

JAMES LUTHER ADAMS' journey to Wellesley Hills began in Ritzville, Washington, where he was born in 1901. His father was a farmer and a fundamentalist Baptist preacher who opposed his son's getting an education; he believed it would destroy James' faith. Eventually James attended the University of Minnesota and graduated in 1924. While an undergraduate he felt himself tugged between the passion he felt for religious institutions and what they could accomplish and his rejection of organized religion in most forms. When told that the Unitarian minister in Minneapolis, the Reverend John Dietrich, might be a good person to talk with, he sought Dietrich out and became convinced he might find the freedom to chart his own religious journey in Unitarianism. James enrolled in Harvard Divinity School and graduated in 1927.

Adams had always appreciated choral singing, whether he embraced the faith expressed in the lyrics or not. He particularly remembered one night after singing the *Bach Mass in B Minor* with the Harvard Glee Club under Serge Koussevitzky at Symphony Hall in Boston: "A renewed conviction came over me that here in the mass beginning with the 'kyrie' and proceeding through the 'crucifixus' to the 'Agnus Dei' and 'Dona nobis pacem,' all that was essential in the human and the divine was expressed. My love of the music awakened in me a profound sense of gratitude to Bach for having displayed as through a prism and in a way that was irresistible for me, the essence of Christianity."

After drifting away from the Christian tradition in the direction of a highly intellectual and humanistic philosophy of life, Adams found that his love of the Christian tradition, though not the Christianity taught by his parents, was given back to him through Bach.

Adams was still ambivalent about Christianity in its institutional form, and he recalled the moment that helped to resolve this ambivalence. He saw Samuel McChord Crothers, minister of the First Parish Church in Cambridge, checking a book out of Widener Library at Harvard. He had always wanted to meet this man. So he introduced himself, telling Crothers that he was thinking of becoming a professor rather than going into the ministry, "whereupon he [Crothers] said the contacts between a professor and his students are generally more casual than substantial." Crothers added:

> I have been minister of First Parish for thirty years, and I am now performing weddings of people whom I initially christened. I saw them through Sunday school, and in one way or another I was in touch with them through high school and college. There is no profession that I know of that offers this kind or continuity and depth. It is true that some serious-minded people attempt to find a surrogate for the kind of church of which I am speaking by joining groups concerned with adult education or civic interests. These associations, however, are evanescent in contrast to a church with its pastoral and educational benefits.

After graduation from Harvard in 1927, Adams became minister of the Second Church in Salem, Massachusetts. He was a young, interesting man with more than the usual amount of energy for taking on new tasks. Among other things, he supported the striking workers of the Pequot Mills and established a clearly defined activist profile in the town.

In 1933 he intrigued the Wellesley Hills congregation in his candidacy for their minister. Unfortunately, their financial prospects were not as good as they had been. In an April 18, 1933, letter to the congregation, the finance committee chair reported that of the eighty-four families who contributed in 1932, their combined contributions this year were nine percent less. While eleven families who did not pledge in 1932 did pledge in 1933, forty-eight families who pledged in 1932 had not yet responded. The total pledged to date was over $2,500 less than the same total last year.

The finance chair went on to say, "This has presented a very difficult and discouraging task to the Standing Committee in the preparation of a budget." The areas most likely to be cut were the church school, music, and the minister's salary. The minister's salary had been cut ten percent in the previous year and likely would be cut by almost $1,100 this year.

It was a difficult time for a minister to be considering a move or for a church to be attempting to attract a new minister. As Adams explained in his autobiography, "Over the years I had grown fond of my [Salem] flock, by sharing their difficult times. Yet I felt drawn to accept the offer at the Wellesley Hills church because of its reputation. Not only was it one of the largest Unitarian churches in New England, but as a parish it was also well known for its civic involvement as well as its literary and artistic organizations. Moreover, it had one of the largest Sunday schools in the Unitarian denomination." Adams was installed as minister of the Wellesley Hills church on March 4, 1934.

A month or so later, the Standing Committee's annual report stated, "During the year at the suggestion of your minister, the Committee of Church Life has been formed. This committee of 14 members, for the most part husbands and wives, already has made some excellent suggestions and promises well to contribute in a material way to a broader and richer life within the church."

The report goes on to point out that the Sunday school, which has grown from 165 children to 230 since Katherine Hall had taken over the superintendence, has more lately become a worry because Mrs. Hall has had to resign that role to be part-time parish assistant and full-time mother. It adds, "We believe this problem definitely ties in with the difficulties of the minister who now is overburdened with a tremendous amount of time-consuming details. With 300 families now on the parish list and with many new ones constantly moving to Wellesley, the minister has a hopeless task in trying to make proper contacts in the direction of making and keeping new members for our church."

The Standing Committee report then suggests putting a religious education professional in the role, something that was being done increasingly by other congregations in the denomination. This, the report further suggests, will enable the minister to more effectively go about his parish duties. The report concludes by recommending what we today call a "reach" budget—particularly considering what the report refers to as "this so-called depression." The report is optimistic not only about the economy but also about the ability of the parish to rise to this occasion. It concludes, "Under our minister's able and enthusiastic leadership, the new year augers well for a more widespread interest and active participation in church affairs. With many new members being added to our numbers and with the full cooperation and participation of all of its members, our church is bound to widen and deepen its sphere of influence for individual and collective benefit."

In his year-end report of 1934-35, Adams details that morning services were held on forty-three Sundays, and he had preached on thirty-six of them. The church school has been divided; a junior church of children ages ten to sixteen worships separately from the adults on Sunday morning with Adams preaching most often along the lines of his sermon to the adults that Sunday. Fifty-five children have been added to the church school census not counting those added to the cradle roll. Numerous meetings for teachers have been held to orient them to a new curriculum. Adams' wife Margaret has taken on a major role in keeping things sane.

Rev. James Luther Adams

Several discussion groups were held at the parsonage including one on religion and literature and another on central religious beliefs. Adams reports making 510 parish calls that year, mostly on new people. Even though Adams has always been known for his energy, 510 parish calls along with the other activities he proposes seems a little over the top.

Adams' 510 parish calls are reminiscent of a story in the area about the minister of a neighboring parish who racked up an unimaginable number of parish visits. When asked how he accomplished this he replied, "Two or three times a week I start strolling down Main Street in my village. There is a restaurant at the head of the street, and I stop there first, not leaving until I have spoken to all of the diners. I proceed to the fire station and talk to all of the firemen there, two of whom are members of my parish. I go down through all of the shops, meeting and talking with the people I meet there or pass on the street. Every person spoken to counts as a parish call."

Adams reports a number of cases of acute pastoral need, some of which required a great deal of time and effort. He has also been involved with Unitarian ministers and laymen trying to create an order of worship that many congregations would see as a useful improvement. He also mentions his work on the American Unitarian Association's Commission of Appraisal and concludes his report with these words: "All of these activities, I believe, have added something to the life of our own parish and to my own usefulness through the new direction and confidence that have come as a result of finding common ground with numerous other Unitarian churches and their ministers."

Adams' work on the Commission of Appraisal requires some background. As president of the American Unitarian Association, the Reverend Samuel Atkins Eliot had brought the AUA from a small staff of four to a staff of twenty-five. It had moved from publishing pamphlets and keeping track of ministers to serving more like the headquarters of a young and growing religious movement. Many of the promotional efforts that worked for the Wellesley congregation had been in response to Eliot's initiatives. But in 1927, he resigned from his leadership of the AUA and became minister of the Arlington Street Church in Boston.

Several movements and events over the next few years dramatically shaped the situation that his successor, the Reverend Louis Cornish, would confront. These included the Great Depression, the rise of fascism in Europe, and a prolonged uncertainty about the future of religious values as typified in the "humanist controversy." Congregations that had not historically had much energy became even less energetic as much of the denomination along with the nation fell into a general malaise. The departed Samuel Eliot had been a force of nature. Cornish, the new president, was a fine parish minister but did not have the institutional vision of Eliot and spent much of his effort maintaining ties with liberal congregations in other countries.

In May of 1934, Kenneth McDougal, the Standing Committee chair in Wellesley Hills, wrote to the *Christian Register*, the AUA's denominational publication, "Neither today nor for several years past have we . . . had a program worthy of our tradition and opportunities. . . . We drift, we play with such naïve notions as putting 100,000 Unitarians to work. . . . We . . . content ourselves with exchanges of good will with a group of liberal Filipinos. . . . We are known less and less as a pioneering and prophetic church. . . . Let there be for the Association a commission of appraisal." As it happened, the annual meeting of Unitarians—then known as May Meetings—was taking place in Boston, and a Commission of Appraisal was established on May 22, 1934.

From 1934 to 1937, the primary issue for Unitarians concerned about institutional maintenance was survival. However, in 1937 Frederick May Eliot, the chair of the Commission of Appraisal, wrote, "It is time for Unitarians to adopt the adjective 'aggressive' in thinking and talking about their denominational program—especially in the field of church extension. We can have an aggressive policy without irrelevance or arrogance or bad manners; and the risk of being misunderstood is less than the risk of being overlooked. . . . The results of this part of our program will determine the whole question of our future."

Adams remembered that he and McDougal started with a series of meetings with lay leaders and ministers in the Wellesley Hills minister's study—now the chapel. Then they traveled up and down the East Coast visiting prominent lay leaders to get them behind this new effort and to get a sense of what they were learning.

The result of their work was a lengthy report titled "Unitarians Face a New Age." It made specific recommendations for turning the situation around and proved to be vital reading for every minister and active layperson. Perhaps most significantly it brought Frederic May Eliot greater exposure and recognition, which led to his being elected next AUA president to preside over the post-war growth that led to a more active religious movement.

One of the most provocative questions the commission asked was, "Could Unitarians say what they believed, or were beliefs among us so diverse as to defy being articulated in one statement?" They believed that such a statement could be made if both agreements and tensions were set forth and if all statements were regarded as tentative. They saw the lines of such a statement forming as follows:

Unitarians agree:

1. in affirming the primacy of the free exercise of intelligence in religion, believing that in the long run the safest guide to Truth is human intelligence.

2. in affirming the paramount importance for the individual of his own moral convictions and purposes.

3. in affirming that the social implications of religion are indispensable to its vitality and validity as expressed in terms of concern for social conditions and the struggle to create a just social order.

4. in affirming the importance of the church as the organized expression of religion.

5. in affirming the necessity of worship as a deliberate effort to strengthen the individual's grasp as the highest spiritual values of which he is aware.

6. in affirming the national nature of the universe.

Unitarians disagree:

1. as to the expediency of using the traditional vocabulary of religion, within a fellowship which includes many who have rejected the ideas commonly associated with words such as "God," "prayer," "communion," "salvation," "immortality."

2. as to the wisdom of maintaining a definitely Christian tradition, and the traditional forms of Christian worship.

3. as to the religious values of a purely naturalistic philosophy.

4. as to the adequacy and competence of man to solve his own problems, both individual and social.

5. as to the advisability of direct action by churches in the field of social and political problems.

Contemporary Unitarian Universalists may notice that these statements are fairly primitive when compared with the current Unitarian Universalist Purposes and Principles and reflect that the denomination has come quite a distance in the eighty years since this earliest statement. The effort was started in Wellesley Hills and guided along the way by its minister, Rev. James Luther Adams.

Wakeup calls are often resented and sometimes ignored by many people. To be effective in our denomination, they need to come either from a source that is credible to many people or a congregation that is recognized as successful. Adams was not considered one of our leading ministers at this time, but the congregation he served was defying all of the norms of defeat and decline that beset the Unitarian denomination, and that push gave credibility to the commission.

During Adams' short ministry, his early sermon titles included:

Thunderclaps and the Visible Upsets of Grace

The Achievement of Leisure

Keeping Friendships in Repair

Spiritual Pilfering

The Bridge of Confidence

The Myth of Individualism

Religion vs. Culture

The Uses of Adversity

The Discovery of Satan

I have met Jim Adams, heard him preach, spent several hours talking with him, and researched his works. His scholarly background augured the career he would later have as a very effective lecturer. He had a dry wit, a keen ear for interesting stories and examples, and an encyclopedic memory for what he read or heard. His students loved him and often attended informal talks he and his wife Margaret hosted in their Cambridge home. I have no doubt that many in the Wellesley congregation also loved his warmth, his energy, and his clever play with ideas. During my ministry in Wellesley, I met many who spoke of him in precisely that way, though I am sure there were others who were less enthralled with this young know-it-all from Harvard.

On September 8, 1935, Adams sent a letter to the congregation in which he explained that the death of Professor Clayton Bowen of Meadville Theological School, then one of the leading sources of Unitarian ministers, had opened up a position that was being offered to him as professor of Christian institutions. Taking such a position would enable him to pursue his concerns about the nature of the church and its response to contemporary society, and he had accepted it. Clearly aware of the surprise, regret, and very possibly anger with which this letter would be received, he concluded with these words:

> It is with keen regret that I must sever my present relationship with the people of this parish. In the church school, in the various organizations of the church and in the church itself, Mrs. Adams and I have found warmth of friendship, warmth of loyalty and a

vitality, which we know from experience to be rare and perhaps never to be encountered again. We are, as many of you know, also persuaded that this parish in its institutional life is one possessing the greatest promise in this section of the denomination, and we look forward confidently with you to its rapid growth and constantly increasing effectiveness. . . .

It is said that ambassador Joseph A. Choate once was asked what one highest thing he would wish if permitted to have his heart's desire. His reply was that he would like above all to be Mrs. Choate's second husband. If I should ever return to the professional work of the ministry again, and were permitted to have my heart's desire, I should ask that I be allowed to become my own successor at the Unitarian Society of Wellesley Hills. But whether or not that boon is ever granted I shall, since I am leaving the active ministry, beg leave of you and your next minister to allow me to think of you, in some special sense as my parish.

Adams actually persuaded Meadville to grant him a leave of absence to tour Europe where he studied the rise of fascism in European institutions and the effectiveness of those institutions in combating it. He returned with a treasure of homemade movies and his own commentary, which gave many liberals their first thoughtful assessment of what was happening and perhaps of what could have stopped it.

Adams taught at Meadville Theological School, then at Harvard, and finally at Andover Newton Theological School. At the Meadville library on winter nights, the furnace's hot air blowing up through the cold stacks caused a great deal of creaking and groaning. New seminarians who were studying late in the library heard these sounds and became very uneasy. They were told by those who had gone before them that it was the ghost of James Luther Adams [who was still alive, actually] searching the stacks for a book he had not yet read.

CHAPTER 12

The Minister as Prophet

THE WELLESLEY HILLS ministerial search committee had met a minister from the British Unitarian Association in 1936 who seemed as if he might be perfect for the job in Wellesley. Members of the committee even went to Britain to see if this man could be persuaded to come to Wellesley and be the minister there. The candidate could not see his way clear to leaving his native land at a time when it might well come under attack.

The next minister on their list was the Reverend Waitstill Hastings Sharp who must have seemed as if he had been bred for the job. He began his ministry in Wellesley in August of 1936.

Sharp was born in Boston on May 1, 1902. His father, Dallas Lore Sharp, had been a poet and professor of English at Boston University for twenty-five years. Grace Hastings Sharp, his mother, was descended from New England ancestors who had trekked west to Ohio.

Waitstill grew up in Hingham and attended the Old Ship Unitarian Church with his parents. He graduated from Boston University in 1923 and from Harvard Law School in 1926. During these latter studies he taught church school at the Second Church of

Boston. With the help of the Second Church's minister, he was later promoted to director of religious education for the American Unitarian Association. He married Martha Ingram Dickie on Star Island, New Hampshire, in 1927. He then served as a parish minister in Meadville, Pennsylvania, from 1933 until 1936.

Sharp was not the only Wellesley Unitarian minister who had spent time in Meadville either as local pastor or earlier as a student at Meadville Theological School before it moved to Chicago. Albert Vorse also served the Meadville church, which had a history of being a pioneer for religious liberalism in its region.

It is also worth remembering that before he left, James Luther Adams had recommended that the congregation hire both a religious education professional and of course a new parish minister. It is not likely that he intended they should saddle the minister, no matter how qualified in religious education, with both major responsibilities. But this was the middle of the depression, and the congregation was not optimistic about making its budget.

In the 1936 Standing Committee report to the congregation, Luna Niles wrote:

> Last August the unexpected resignation of Mr. Adams, called away to a larger field of service in Unitarianism, was a severe blow. During the leaderless period that followed, the patient and loyal cooperation of our parish has been deeply appreciated. This spirit, so clearly shown during the last several months, represents a real basis for optimism for the future of our parish and the individual gain that must surely come from close association with it.
>
> During Mr. Adams' absence our church school superintendent and parish assistant have carried on under trying conditions. Handicapped by having been with us but a short time, his earnest but devoted efforts have contributed greatly toward our various activities now being in excellent position to go strongly ahead under the new leadership of our Mr. Sharp.

At this point special mention should be made of the work of the Pulpit committee. The selection of Mr. Sharp was certainly an inspired choice. We are indeed fortunate in having Mr. and Mrs. Sharp with us. Active participation by a larger number of our members is all that is necessary to assure for us a stronger church, influential for greater good. Under the able and inspired leadership of Mr. Sharp, we believe this happy state will soon come to pass.

Waitstill wrote this response to the annual meeting:

The story of my relationship with the church is brief. On Sunday, January 19, 1936, Mr. Henry S. Bothfeld and Mr. Harold L. Niles appeared in Meadville, Pennsylvania, and proposed that we consider transferring our services to this town. On Sunday, February 16, I preached here. On Tuesday, February 25, this parish voted a call and extended it by long distance telephone, which I accepted orally at the time, confirming by a letter on February 27 in reply to a formal letter received that day from Mr. Bothfeld. On Sunday, March 1, I resigned my pastorate at Meadville, conducting the final service there on Sunday, March 29. We arrived in your hospitable midst on April 1, 1936.

The minister elect and his wife wish to take this occasion formally, but nonetheless sincerely, to record two feelings which need a more ample vocabulary than ours for full expression: (1) their sense of honor and the hopefulness of this church in extending them a call to its ministry. You have summoned us to this post in the faith that we shall rise to the occasion of its leadership. We have accepted in the faith that you desire this to be a revered and serviceable outpost of modern religious belief. We pledge you the best that in us lies, asking only your support and help when we call for it on behalf of our common cause—this society of faith. We promise you our full relationship and constant devotion to this enterprise, and we will undertake only those denominational and community works that serve its best welfare. This is our pledge. We leave to each of you severally the substances of your own implicit pledges.

(2) In the second place we wish to record our gratitude to all concerned in providing the beauty and the comfort of the parsonage. We arrived in days of pouring spring rain and forever will recall the loveliness and warmth and cleanliness of our new home. The readiness of the house and the hospitality of those whose guests we were and the kindness of those who sent flowers and food to start us off, made up a perfect welcome. So we have felt unanimously desired from the start.

These words, though heartfelt, do seem a little stiff. Could this be partly a result of Sharp's law education, or could it be an expression of his personality as well? Perhaps it was a bit of both. New Englanders, even then, anticipated that their new minister might and perhaps ought to be a bit reserved, preserving for himself some dignity that he and they felt his role required. Yet they also liked to see some semblance of warmth and personality.

However, church member Marion Niles wrote her memories of Sharp, "Our church was most fortunate for eight memorable years with Waitstill Sharp. He continued to work with the young people of the church, often with two different groups in the parsonage on Sunday evenings. He brought to the pulpit the problems of the day, but he did it as someone said with a radiancy, which made it inspiring. Members often lingered on the church steps after the service for interesting discussions."

Here are some of Waitstill's sermon topics that were mentioned in the *Wellesley Townsman*:

What's a Conscience Between Friends?

Another War for Democracy

Letting Your Neighbor's Conscience Do Its Work

Render unto Caesar the Things That Are God's

The Marks of a Great Church

The Wellesley parishioners were surely in little doubt as to Sharp's politics. Any remaining doubt would have fled upon the news that Sharp was appointed chairman of the Wellesley Peace Action Committee. In November of 1937, the church hosted an armistice remembrance service consisting of young people from most of the town's congregations led by their ministers.

Sharp's sermons had apparently also drawn students from both Wellesley College and Babson College. On November 12, 1937, the church held a college students breakfast followed by a church service. The efforts over the years to enlist college students in church events are legion, and most left a remnant of good will. Even so, many college students, then and now, are not likely to seek out a Unitarian church that is several miles from campus.

Rev. Waitstill Hastings Sharp

In 1938 the Unitarian Society and the Hills Congregational Church joined in a partnership to sponsor a forum on the subject "The Spiritual Principles Underlying the Function of a Newspaper as an Organ of Public Opinion." This was part of an effort sponsored throughout the country by the congregations of the American Unitarian Association. A few nights later newspapermen were invited to gather to express their views of the role of newspaper journalism.

The *Wellesley Townsman*, which splashed news of Republican candidates across the front page and refused to accept news of the Democrats, responded in an editorial, "We feel that great good was accomplished by this get together of editors and laymen. It offered newspapermen an opportunity of presenting their aims, ambitions, trials and tribulations to people who were eager to learn and to listen. It afforded the laymen an opportunity of asking questions in regard to the newspaper policies. And through this medium it was possible for each side to acquire a better understanding of one another's problems and must have tended to iron out possible misunderstandings which otherwise might never have been misunderstood."

During this year and the next, Sharp preached several times in different ways on the values and disciplines of democracy. While this might seem like a sermon favorable to "motherhood," we need to remember that democracy at this time was being questioned in Italy, Germany, and throughout the world. For those who did not see or anticipate the perils of the new fascist governments, democracy may have seemed like an awkward, unwieldy way of getting things done while iron-fisted leadership did seem to "make the trains run on time." To tell a congregation that democratic government requires something of an act of faith was a prophetic stance then and needed to be done more than once. One of Sharp's sermon titles suggests his drift: "When Evil Wins a Victory What Shall Christians Do?"

In March of that year just before Easter, Sharp presented five evening lectures on "The Life of Christ." The announcement of this series said, "Those who heard his lectures on the prophets last year will know he is a stimulating speaker."

However good they felt about their minister and the work he was doing, the depression ground on and was affecting both the income and the savings of members of the congregation. The congregation had come up with a deficit of about $800 for the yearly budget. They were behind on paying off loans to the American Unitarian Association and to a local bank that had been undertaken to finance construction of the parish hall. When most congregations are in such a situation, the usual suspects to suffer drastic reductions are music and religious education. David Hall, chair of the music committee, wrote the following:

> Under the present budget, two courses are open to the Music Committee. 1) We can do away entirely with the choir and rely on the organ supplemented entirely with occasional volunteer instrumental music. If this is the desire of the church let us know herewith. 2) We believe, however, that choir music is such a time bound part of a church service that most of you would appreciate the best we can do furnishing such music. This second course is the one that has been adopted. Again, I say if we are mistaken in guessing your wishes let us know about it. Your music committee is aware that church music can be as disturbing as any of the things that disturb churchgoers. We are anxious to please and therefore [welcome] any and all constructive comments. You may be interested to know that it has already been suggested that we use a Victrola in place of the choir and that we pay $10 a Sunday for a fine baritone soloist.
>
> Perhaps, unfortunately, paying soloists is out of the question. On the other hand we are blessed by having no soloist. The choir of necessity has the virtues and weaknesses of a volunteer choir. Out of this parish of two or three hundred members, the number truly interested in making a joyful noise unto the Lord is seldom more than a dozen and frequently as few as six. Times are hard. Under the circumstances the results are not always as polished as we would like to have them.
>
> Type of music being sung is such as has stood the test of times. It is sturdy enough to survive and has stood the test of the times no matter what we or any other choir may do to it. We are fortunate enough to have the services of a musician possessing the good taste that Mr. Tuttle has. I think this matter of taste will not be fully appreciated until some day, somewhere, you happen to notice its absence.
>
> Please remember that this is your music committee. You can help first by making your comments direct to the music committee.

They should be informed of what you want if you are sure yourselves what it is. Any suggestions for $10 baritones should be accompanied by a check. Secondly you can help by singing in the choir yourself, or by not singing as the case may be. . . . If you won't sing or won't endow a baritone, interest someone else in doing so. Perhaps you can persuade the young people to reinforce the faithful veterans.

Finally if you don't like the way the choir sounds perhaps some of you have some old rugs that we could put on the floor of the choir loft to deaden the sound.

It appears that musical tastes differed as widely in the Wellesley Unitarian Society in 1937 as they have before and since, as is true in most of our congregations. Where differences become rigid, as perhaps they do from time to time, sometimes humor helps leaven the discussion as David Hall attempts here.

From 1938 and for several years, the church records seem to have been more carefully kept. We learn that in that year another special fund drive was needed to reduce the operating deficit. The result was ninety-three people contributing $5,800, or $1,400 less than the desired goal. This enabled the Society to pay back its two loans a bit more and to make some—but by no means all—of the needed repairs on the buildings. Standing Committee Chair Marion Niles wrote:

One is impressed with the friendly cooperative spirit that has permeated all of the works of the church—the courage to meet difficult situations and a vitality that is rich in promise for the future. At the moment we are in that in-between period facing the loss of many of our loyal workers, of deeply rooted traditions and looking forward to the strength which will come from this large young group with its potential power and resources, but many without those traditions. There is need of more frequently bringing before us all of the problems of the church—not saving them all for one annual meeting. Why not two meetings during the year—for it is only by our united and cooperative facing of the problems and opportunities of the church that the successful carrying on can be achieved and the realization of the actual and unsuspected values.

As a side note, the laymen and women who lead our congregations deserve great appreciation. Typically, twenty to twenty-five percent of the members of a congregation step forward and bear the responsibilities for finding solutions that will work for the institution of the church and more or less meet with the approval or acceptance of most of the congregation. Congregations may have ministers who were good fits for the position, some who were adequate for the position, and some who were a misfit for the pastorate they held. Throughout these fortunate and unfortunate transitions, there is a core of people who hold the whole thing together.

Throughout these pages we have heard and will hear their visions of how their religious faith might inspire others, how their congregation might galvanize their community, and how all things are possible if we only pull together. They know, of course, that for eighty percent of their congregation, the church is not a source of their unwavering loyalty but another institution competing for their attention. Nonetheless, those who accept the leadership push on and prove their commitment over and over. Without this leadership core in Wellesley Hills, there would be no continuity down through the years and no history to write. All of that said, we are about to enter what may have been the toughest time in the history of the Unitarian Society of Wellesley Hills.

CHAPTER 13

Unitarian Minister Declares War on Hitler

SUNDAY AFTERNOONS WERE particularly difficult times for ministers in those days. Coming off an emotional high of preaching and then sharing social time with their congregations, ministers frequently had to meet with one or two youth groups and call on a few shut-ins before being able to write an end to the work day, relax, and put their feet up. It was precisely at the end of such a Sunday afternoon in the winter of 1938 that Waitstill Sharp got a call from Everett Baker, vice president of the American Unitarian Association who now lived in Wellesley. Could Waitstill and Martha come over for a few minutes? In those days if the deputy head of your denomination called and asked to see you right away, you went. So they got a sitter for their two young children, Hastings and Martha Content, and went to see what Baker wanted.

The AUA wanted a Unitarian minister and his wife to sail to Europe to assist religious and political liberals to escape imprisonment and probable death by the Nazis. The failure of the Munich pact had exposed Hitler's real designs; no one doubted that it was very dangerous to be seen as an enemy of fascist rule. Directly in the path of Nazi aggression, Czechoslovakia had a strong Unitarian community. Norbert Capek led a church of over 1000 members. The community included members of the Maseryk family who were important in the new country's democratic leadership.

Whoever the AUA sent had to have nearly instant credibility in Europe, because they would be dealing with people who had good reason to withhold their trust. This couple would also need to have some stature in the denomination to bring home a report that would be credible to ministers and congregations. Waitstill and Martha, representing one of the fastest growing Unitarian congregations in the country, had that stature. It was also preferable that the AUA's representatives have Anglo-Saxon surnames, giving them standing with the Nazis who were not anxious to take on prominent Americans at this point.

Waitstill asked, "How many other ministers have you offered this chance to?" The answer was seventeen. Seventeen colleagues had turned down this opportunity either because they did not want to derail successful careers, leave their congregations, or leave their families. Something like this does not stay secret for long. The likelihood is that Waitstill knew this request might come to him, but it is doubtful that Martha knew. In any case, neither of them knew what they would decide together.

"What about my church?" Sharp asked. Baker volunteered that he would make sure preaching and pastoral responsibilities were adequately covered. The question of who might take care of the children was more difficult. Hastings was three years old, and Martha Content was an infant. Edna Stebbins, an old family friend known as "Aunt Edna" to the children, offered to care for them. This task was made easier for all because Alice, the Sharp's maid, had played a significant role in raising them and would be staying on. With this last concern covered, the Sharps decided to approach the congregation's leadership.

Shortly thereafter, in January of 1939, Robert Dexter and Everett Baker, representing the AUA, presented a request that the church extend Waitstill Sharp a leave of absence from February 1 to September 1 to administer a relief fund in Czechoslovakia. This would be a leave without compensation unless the church came out of the year with a surplus. At an informal meeting of the parish after church the next Sunday, this leave was granted.

In her annual report to the congregation as Standing Committee chair, Marion Niles wrote:

> The crisis in the church came with a request made by the A.U.A. for the granting of a leave of absence for our minister that he and his wife might accept the Quaker-Unitarian mission for service in Czechoslovakia for seven months. Within twenty-four hours a full committee meeting had granted the request subject to the approval of the parish which was granted on the following Sunday. At the next two meetings of the Standing Committee plans were made for the carrying on of the church in the absence of the Minister. Dr. Everett M. Baker took entire charge of the preaching schedule. A small emergency committee was appointed with Marion H. Niles as Chairman. Mrs. Curtis Hilliard and Professor Thomas Sherwood were appointed to act between the meetings of the Standing Committee. Mr. Donald Woods of Tufts College was appointed as upper church school director. Mrs. Kenneth McDougal has taken charge of the weekly calendar. . . . I cannot speak too warmly of the willingness and the helpfulness, which has always marked Miss Hunter's office hours in the parish house. Mr. Sherwood, as chairman of religious education, has given every Sunday to the attendance at the church school and a survey of the school and its needs.
>
> The spirit of cooperation has been remarkable. We have carried on. We have heard distinguished preachers, but I think it has been at a distinct sacrifice—it could not be otherwise, a sacrifice

of which we are all especially conscious at this time of our Annual Meeting when we need the inspiration and help of our church leader. But with this sense of sacrifice is also the consciousness that our little church is through its minister and his wife helping perhaps in no small way to perform a great humanitarian service to a tragically broken people. This absence has taught us all a fuller realization of the infinite detail of a minister's life and of that of his wife, exacting daily patience and tolerance.

What did it take for a congregation to give up its minister to an unsettled situation in Europe on the brink of war? It is a complicated picture. Isolationist sentiment in the United States remained strong until the bombing of Pearl Harbor on December 7, 1941. Franklin Roosevelt would run for his third term in office on the grounds that he would not take the country into war. It is not at all clear that members of the Wellesley Hills congregation realized at first that their minister and his wife would be keeping just a few steps ahead of the Gestapo and at the end of their first trip would narrowly miss getting arrested, which might have meant their disappearing forever. For those who realized even part of what was happening or going to happen, it took a great deal of courage.

When the Nazis invaded Prague, Czechoslovakia, the Sharps were there. They were desperately trying to convince refugees to come out of hiding long enough to flee. The Sharps' phones were tapped, their files secretly rifled. Taxi drivers were often members of the Gestapo, which meant that Waitstill or Martha could never take a taxi where they actually wanted to go; instead, they took it to a different address, got out, pretended to go to that address, and then walked to their actual destination. Strangers were automatically suspect. Were the people seeking the help that you were sent there to give, or were they compiling evidence that would eventually harm you? Almost certainly some of their parishioners realized the magnitude of the risk the Sharps were undertaking and yet approved the mission.

According to the *Jerusalem Post* many years later, "The Unitarian Church was already a step in front of the Nazis having set up a secretive network of volunteers and agencies to secure the safe passage of Jews and non-Jews out of Prague." The task became even more difficult when the Nazis entered Prague on March 15, 1939. For the first five months, the Sharps continued their work undaunted by the presence of the Gestapo or the danger of being arrested. In August 1939, the couple left Prague and headed back to the United States.

Martha and Rev. Waitstill Sharp

They were enthusiastically welcomed back and were glad to be back.

Back in Wellesley, the church school at the Unitarian Society had been the source of continuing discussion and occasionally argument. Traditionally the minister had been charged with the responsibility of keeping his "scholars" quiet and his teachers happy; but as enrollment grew to well over 200, the job was simply becoming too large for the Society to continue to fool itself into thinking that a well-intentioned lay person or even the minister could handle it. In June of 1939, the religious education committee proposed to the board that they hire Mrs. Russell "Betty" Baker as the first professional director of religious education the church would have.

Betty Baker was a leader among her peer religious educators. She was born into the Universalist movement and received a graduate education at the Universalist divinity school at St. Lawrence University. She ran a taut but warm church school. Having served one congregation before coming to Wellesley Hills, she loved the children in her care but held high standards for them. When she died in 2001, several people who had grown up in her White Plains church school reflected that she had taught them the importance of having a church by teaching them to respect who they were and the faith that gathered them together.

In a professional autobiography written in 1985, Betty Baker wrote this description of the Wellesley Hills church in 1939:

> The chairman of the board was Linwood Chase, Dean of Boston University Graduate School of Education; The R.E. chairman was Everett Moore Baker, Vice President of the American Unitarian Association, a marvelous man and an exceptional administrator. He taught me what was to become one of my greatest strengths – administration. One of the members of the R.E. Committee was Kay Durrell, the wife of Donald Durrell who was pioneering in remedial reading. . . .

> School systems did not [then] have remedial reading specialists. But because of Dr. Durrell I was aware of the personality destruction that inability to read produces. And so I entered Boston University to study diagnosis and treatment of reading disability. With the approval of my R.E. chairman and the Board I devoted a great deal of my time to religious education through remedial reading diagnosis and tutoring.

With Waitstill and Betty Baker now in stride in September of 1939, it felt to the congregation as though things were back to normal.

It felt that way to the Sharps as well, and they were relieved. Despite the loving care their children received during Waitstill and Martha's absence, the Sharp kids were still quite young to have their parents gone for several months. They had worried about what might have happened to their parents, and they were too young to have really understood the explanations they were given. They were not in great shape emotionally.

Meanwhile, the group Waitstill and Martha had nurtured into existence to support their work, now called at Waitstill's suggestion the Unitarian Service Committee, was formed and officially recognized. The Wellesley Hills congregation made the first contribution to the Service Committee's ongoing support. Jean Powell, the young daughter of a member of the congregation, walked that first contribution down the aisle of a AUA General Assembly to considerable applause; that image lingered throughout the years in the minds of many of my parishioners as a source of great pride.

Though Waitstill and Martha were home and glad to be so, they were distinctly aware of the situation they had left behind in Europe. In his Memorial Day sermon in May of 1939, Waitstill declared war on Nazi Germany, generating the *Boston Globe* headline, "Wellesley Pastor Urges U.S. To Declare War On Germany." In a tightly reasoned sermon he said that we have waited long enough, and any further delay will only create further problems. No doubt many members of his congregation agreed with him, but how they felt about he and Martha walking again into the jaws of this conflict will never be entirely clear.

Eventually, Waitstill got another phone call from the AUA. They needed him and Martha to go back to Europe. The Sharps thought they had already given a great deal at some considerable sacrifice to their family and its life together. They had promised the children a full family summer vacation on a New Hampshire lake with undistracted parents. But the AUA persisted, and there was more than a hint that turning this offer down might negatively impact Waitstill's future professional career. As it turned out, the AUA had already contacted the Wellesley church board and obtained their permission to grant Waitstill a leave of absence from June 15, 1940, to the first Sunday in October.

The situation of Western relief workers in Europe was now considerably more dire because the German Wehrmacht had marched over Denmark and Norway, Belgium and Holland, and finally the northern part of France. Southern France was occupied by a French fascist government which was tolerated for a while by the Nazi regime and cooperated with them off and on.

The Sharps set up an office in Lisbon, Portugal, and Nazi spies watched heavily what they were doing. The Nazis knew that anyone seeking to escape the roundup might very well try to escape through Portugal. The stakes were much higher now since those who failed to get out—Jews and political enemies of fascism particularly—were likely to be sent to the camps to die. Working in this situation required a great deal of wit and considerable bravery. Many years later Waitstill and Martha would be recognized as "Righteous Among the Nations" at Yad Vashem, the Holocaust remembrance center, by the nation of Israel for putting their lives on the line frequently to help people escape the Nazi roundup. The Sharps are two of only five Americans to be accorded this honor.

At the 1940 annual meeting of the Wellesley congregation, Thomas Sherwood, chair of the Standing Committee, reported:

> To say that the year has been one of healthy growth for the church is to understate the case very considerably. We have grown almost too rapidly, for continued growth at the same rate for five years would tax our building facilities and we might be tempted to build another parish house. Mr. and Mrs. Sharp were missed, particularly in the late spring, but their return on Labor Day enabled us to

welcome them home and to share in their exciting and significant work in Czechoslovakia. By preparing and presenting a series of lectures on their work abroad they benefitted the church financially, but the indirect benefit to the church from the wide interest in their work has been much more important.

Mr. and Mrs. Sharp have continued their vigorous and successful refugee work through the winter although it involved much extra effort and work from both of them. We have been proud to have ministers who overwork for such good purpose although concerned at times lest they sacrifice health. In retrospect it is evident that the Sharp's mission to Central Europe was a thorough going success, and we are proud to have had a small part in it. We feel something like the members of a small golf club whose professional has won a national tournament. Perhaps we should increase our dues.

The average attendance had jumped by thirty percent, and Sherwood believes this is because Waitstill Sharp "has developed a power, a maturity and a depth of understanding which makes him an outstanding preacher." He points out that Betty Baker has created an atmosphere in the church school that has resulted in increased morale. Enrollment is up, attendance has increased, and her salary—viewed as a stretch more than a year ago—now seems more than justified.

Sherwood speaks about the democratic process that allows and sometimes even encourages disagreement. It can work only when each person recognizes that in the nature of things democratic, no one will always get his/her own way all the time. He then continues, "I have been impressed by the extent to which the members of the Society realize this balance of privileges and responsibilities. More than anything else it is this that convinces me that we are on solid ground and that the future holds much in store. More than most church groups we seem to have the ability to keep personalities and imperfections as to detail in a blurred background and focus on the main idea which is that the Christian church is essential and positively must be supported."

Sherwood paraphrased a colleague who described democratic institutions as oases in the midst of an often cruel and uncaring world. He concluded by saying, "You have [here] an oasis. Long may you regard it as holy."

Marion Niles reported for the finance committee that a recent canvass yielded $8,000, an increase of $625 over last year's budget. Despite this news, she said that being in this position can be a little heartbreaking. The fact that twenty percent of the people approached refused to pledge is "staggering." Some have not considered themselves members of the church for some time. Some stated they felt they should pledge to their previous church despite the fact that their children are enrolled in this church school. Some declared they are not quite ready to offer their support and are still thinking about it. Every experienced minister has to deal with this level of disillusionment, usually on the part of a very generous member who because of that generosity is placed in the position of extracting gifts from others and finds that his/her generous spirit is not widely shared.

By the annual meeting of 1941, the Sharps had left again for Europe and come back. Waitstill returned to a congregation that was happy to see him, though perhaps some had quietly voiced reservations about his absences. Waitstill reiterated to them that he had received no salary during either leave of absence.

It may have been difficult for two people who had lived intensely and dangerously in the midst of two war zones to return and get in step with a nation for which the thought of war was still distant. Perhaps that is why Waitstill wrote this section of his annual minister's report:

> In two years we have discovered our power to give to a purpose
> which captures our imagination. . . . But lest we take into ourselves

pride and smugness in this record, and lest we resent further appeals in the near future, let us think about the depth and the extent of the disaster which has overtaken Europe where people just like ourselves—people who have enjoyed the same cultural surroundings which we consider necessary to civilized and happy life—have lost everything: employment, citizenship, all their property of every kind, homes and members of their families. We may rejoice in our record, but so far—both in taxes and in benevolences—we have raised and given only out of our secure abundance. So let us be very sparing in our speaking of the word "sacrifice" [emphasis his]. And let us continue in another year, and even extend the honorable Christian and American tradition of generosity to those in desperate plight. People ought gladly to know and to recognize that participation in a Christian church means giving of self and substance in every possible way.

Later, in speaking of the young people's group at the church, Waitstill returned to issues that would frame his life. He said, "I remember a sentence spoken years ago by Professor Theodore Soares of the University of Chicago. 'No generation has ever succeeded in teaching its children what it did not deeply believe itself' [emphasis his]. There is quite too much of the hypothetical and subjunctive in American suburban life; it is time to recognize some imperatives. The cult of nonchalance is hardly in order when a world is breaking up, and every institution which we believe in is being tested for its life, which is a life in the terms of faithful and understanding believers."

Waitstill concluded by saying, "After the events of these last two months life will go on by one of two roadways. And there are more signs against us at this moment than there are for us. The choice is being hammered out and fought out but behind the willingness of every man in either camp to do or die there glows the spark of faith. Opinions are not meeting on this battlefield—the struggle is between convictions. . . . I who have lived among them have no doubt of the conviction burning in the enemies of our way of life—with what faith shall we qualify—both now in this darkened time . . . and after the first victory is won."

How difficult it must have been to get back to the daily realities of church life, as they then knew it. Waitstill made two recommendations in the midst of this rather powerful report. He renewed his hope that a committee on planning and review be formed. This committee had existed in one form or another throughout several ministers and never quite seemed to achieve a life of its own.

Sharp also renewed a suggestion he had been making for several years for a chancel. This meant that there would be a pulpit on the congregation's left and a lectern on the right. In the middle and against the sanctuary wall would be an altar. Why was this important? In the early meetinghouses the pulpit was front and center because it contained the Bible and from it the word of God was preached. Over a long time, many people began to suspect that it was not the word of God that was being exalted by the central pulpit, but the preacher. To combat this "preacher worship," they suggested separating the pulpit and lectern to separate corners and creating a space—a chancel— where other liturgical functions could take place. The final result would be more like the front of the current Wellesley Hills sanctuary with a lectern in place of the current chalice.

On March 7, 1941, the congregation celebrated the seventieth anniversary of the founding of the church. Their style was a little less "high church" than previous anniversary celebrations, but it included, as the others did not, a time for the children and a sermon about the history of the church given by Waitstill Sharp. He had gathered stories from as many people as he could find about the early years. Without this sermon, titled "Three Score Years and Ten," we might not know even as much as we do today.

Looking at the years leading to 1944, eight issues reappear periodically in the Standing Committee minutes.

War issues: One issue that went away with the end of the war was rationing, particularly of heating oil. This required some consideration of what parts of the church could be used least expensively during cold weather. Another war-related question was air raid shelters. They were created "under the church," presumably in the basement, and Betty Baker was appointed air raid warden.

Parsonage: The parsonage had been on and off the agenda since the beginning. Congregations usually make terrible landlords, and they talked endlessly about possible repair or replacement of each building. It seems the temptation was to think that by selling the current parsonage and buying a cheaper house they could pay off the church debt more quickly. The parsonage in question was directly opposite the church and facing a busy Washington Street. The Standing Committee made the decision to buy a lot on Maugus Avenue and move the existing parsonage around the corner to it. It is not clear from this discussion when Waitstill and Martha Sharp were brought into this decision.

Inclusion: Waitstill did establish the precedent that the minister was to be included in part of each Standing Committee meeting, although they were still careful to make it clear that they could ask him to leave whenever they wanted.

Planning: Waitstill's proposed committee for planning and review was formed as others had been before this time. As had happened before, it served for a while and then dissolved. The usual problem with this committee everywhere seems to be that it is composed of people who can think of ideas that would be great for someone else to implement. In many contemporary congregations such people who plan activities are included on a council and given leadership and decision-making responsibilities.

Music: How to resolve the musical tone of the worship service was an issue back in the 1940s as it has been ever since. Back then there were those who preferred popular tunes, mood music, spirituals, show tunes, or traditional classical music for worship. There is a happy mean, but it is never reached by individuals who dig in their heels and insist that only one genre of music be heard.

Floods: In February of 1944, the lawn just east of the church became a pond, and the church basements flooded probably for some of the same reasons that have been operating ever since.

Name: In the early 1940s, the most concrete effort thus far was launched to change the name of the church to "The Unitarian Church of Wellesley." A member of the Standing Committee wrote the AUA asking if anyone knew why Wellesley was a "society" and not a "church." The response from an AUA functionary was not helpful, suggesting that they just be happy to be a society. The truth is undoubtedly that they are a "society" because the Massachusetts State Legislature would not allow them to be called a "church" when they applied for that change back in the nineteenth century. The legal name is determined by a proposal approved by two-thirds of the congregation that is favorably enacted by the State Legislature. Until then, the legal name is "The Unitarian Society of Wellesley Hills."

Attendance: Periodically every congregation worries about its attendance. There are many more women than men in attendance. There are many more people on the rolls than there are in the pews. There are many more people in the pews or on the rolls than are contributing to the annual budget. These are inevitabilities of congregational life that can be mitigated, but not by preaching at them.

After giving a return to congregational ministry a good run, Waitstill resigned on May 7, 1944, one month before D-Day. He went on to undergo training to work for a United Nations agency for "Relief and Rehabilitation." Meanwhile, he received an offer for the ministry of a very attractive church in Chicago but declined it rather than ask Martha to move again for his career. Waitstill did eventually return to ministry in Davenport, Iowa; Flint, Michigan; and Petersham, Massachusetts.

For the full story of the Sharp's two trips to Europe and more, be sure to read the excellent book *Defying the Nazis: The Sharps' War* by Artemis Joukowsky, the Sharps' grandson.

CHAPTER 14

An Explosion of Numbers

THE STANDING COMMITTEE chairman appointed a pulpit committee of eleven men and women to begin the search for a new minister on May 19, 1944. About a month later, the Standing Committee minutes mentioned talk of the Reverend William Rice as a candidate. In September the pulpit committee shared with the Standing Committee what they were doing and mentioned three ministers of particular interest, none of whom was Bill Rice. A month later the pulpit committee reported two different candidates were under serious consideration. By January of 1945, their leading candidate had turned them down, and there was discussion of either putting the search on hold until the war was over or continuing to search with all deliberate speed.

By May 28, 1945, the pulpit committee chair spoke to the Standing Committee of the "urgent necessity for obtaining a minister, either temporary or permanent." They had gone a year without a minister; apparently new member recruitment and the overall involvement of members in leadership were concerns. Two weeks later, on the last Sunday in June, the committee recommended the Reverend William

B. Rice for congregational consideration. In a letter to the congregation dated June 19, 1945, the pulpit committee wrote:

> Mr. Rice was the unanimous first choice of the Pulpit Committee. For eleven years he has been at the Dover church where he has built a strong society combining the Unitarian and Congregational churches. He has played an important role in denominational affairs as well, being active in the work of the American Unitarian Association as chairman of both the Committee on the Ministry and the Fellowship Committee. He was also the representative of the Ministerial Union on the Board of the A.U.A. In addition to his parish ministry in Dover, Mr. Rice is the Protestant chaplain of the Charles Street Jail in Boston. He is also a member of the National Committee of Army and Navy Chaplains in Washington, D.C.
>
> Mrs. Rice is a graduate of Radcliffe College, and has always participated actively in church work. She was formerly Field Secretary of the Young Peoples Religious Union, and was to have been chairman of this year's summer conference of the National Alliance, had it been held. The Rices have two fine sons, ten and six years old.
>
> Both your Pulpit Committee and your Standing Committee unanimously endorsed and recommend Mr. Rice as the best minister for our church. His wealth of experience, his capacity for working with people, and his well-balanced personality will revitalize our church and bring the kind of leadership we need to make us strong in our community.
>
> We ask you to come and hear Mr. Rice next Sunday morning at ten thirty and plan to attend the short meeting in the Parish House.

At that meeting, Bill Rice was called by the congregation to be the next minister of the church.

In the April 1947 report of the Standing Committee, Chairman J.R. Killiam is enthusiastic about the past year and the prospects for the future. He writes, "The church has made important gains . . . as the treasurer will report. All of our mortgage indebtedness has been extinguished as a result, first of a long series of contributions provided by the Women's Alliance, animated by a determined policy that the church should be debt free and second by the All-Clear Fund Campaign which provided enough additional amount to complete the Debt Clearance program."

With the addition of money from the every-member canvass, $25,000 was raised both to pay off the debt and create a workable budget for the following year. Killiam continues, "The chairman of the Standing Committee feels it appropriate to observe that the current response of the parish and the general financial condition of the church warrant confidence in the steady growth of the Society."

This happy state of affairs gave the Standing Committee and should give the Society reasons to think ahead to some issues that may have been laid aside too long:

- There is an acute need for a larger staff, particularly clerical staff to assist the minister and the director of religious education.
- The growth of the church school only highlights the need for more classrooms and better equipment.
- The idea of creating a chancel has been floating for quite a while, and there was a fund created to make it happen when the financial time was right. That time is now. Killiam points out that members of the congregation should not be startled during the worship services by the crashing sound brought about the collapse of the "archaically interesting but practically defunct furniture" that now populates the chancel.
- A more coordinated form of management is needed, including a church council consisting of the heads of committees— something that had been proposed in one way or another by the last three ministers.

- Additional endowment funds are needed.
- Presenting the church and its minister more vigorously outside the boundaries of Wellesley Hills is important.

In concluding, Killiam expresses his "appreciation to Mr. Rice whose qualities of leadership, administrative skill and moral inspiration have made the committee's work during the past year

Rev. William Brooks Rice

largely one of encouraging, implementing and applauding the ministerial work of this church."

In his annual minister's report, Bill Rice noted the number of weddings, christenings, and funerals at which he officiated. He also pointed out a marked increase in average attendance from 140 the previous church year to 165. He noted that some of this was a reflection of Easter's two worship services attendances at 507 and 590 but more importantly suggested a strong increased interest in the church. He then made a point of thanking the choir and its director for their leadership and "their rich and happy contribution."

Rice also suggested formation of a church fellowship committee made up of men as well as women, reaching out to all Wellesley neighborhoods. He also pointed out that although some people like to go straight home after church, others do not; thus, the church should offer a coffee hour following the service. Many UUs may have thought this coffee hour tradition preceded that of having worship together, but it did not. It was a new idea in 1947.

For several years Bill Rice completed his annual report to the congregation by offering his resignation. He followed this by saying that he was perfectly happy to stay and liked it there, but he wanted the congregation to understand that this was their church and not his. They could vote him out any time they wished. Of course each time they unanimously reaffirmed him as their minister.

The text of Rice's yearly resignation does not call for a secret ballot so that if a loyal or disloyal opposition were to form and vote publically someone would know the size of it and who was in it by this vote. No evidence exists of any other minister following this practice. It is not an advisable practice, although it did no harm to Bill Rice.

At the end of the 1945-46 church year, the congregation numbered 308 adult members and 208 enrolled children—not a great deal more than had been reported the year before. But near the end of the next church year, Rice's first full year, the adult membership was 481 with 235 children enrolled. World War II veterans and their families were moving toward the suburbs. According to the *Wellesley Townsman*, 630 people were added to the Wellesley voting rolls during the next year. Many couples were seeking a moderately liberal church with an optimistic and comparatively undemanding outlook, particularly for their children.

A phrase in the newspaper describes one Wellesley Unitarian service as "one of the popular family Sundays when the children sit with their parents and the auditorium is filled to overflowing." This service also featured the christening of four-and-a-half-year-old Theodore French Parker and three-and-a-half-year-old John Wells Parker, sons of Frank and Katie Parker.

In the December 1948 Standing Committee minutes, a member of the finance committee reports he has analyzed the pledges of the previous year. They broke down as follows:

- $25 or less: 145
- $26 - $50: 71
- $51 - $75: 43
- $76 - $100: 23
- $101 or more: 38
- Same as last year: 98

It is not difficult to surmise that many of these are token pledges intended to hold someone's place in the church school or on the church rolls until such time as the family might become more serious or decide to move on. Factors of this rather ephemeral nature were to become vexing aspects of many Baby Boom congregations that grew to sizes no one ever expected. By the 1965-66 church year, the pledges shrank just as quickly, leaving many ministers and church leaders wondering what they might have done wrong.

Shortly after his arrival, Bill Rice got plenty of favorable attention for something not related to the Wellesley church. Every Sunday afternoon he led the worship service at the Charles Street Jail in Boston. He was also chaplain for that prison population, making himself available during the week for counseling upon request. Rice got the job through Governor Leverett Saltonstall who had been a member of the Dover church while Rice was its minister.

Most of the prisoners in the jail were there for the period between their arrest and trial, but Rice seemed to have gotten to know them well and, for some, to have earned their confidence. He believed most had grown up without the advantages that suburban children have, and in this deficit lay some of the reasons for their drifting into a life of crime. Be that as it may, Chandler Gregg, the man who frequently went with him to provide musical accompaniment for the worship services and who was the church's director of music during my twenty-three-year term as minister, once told me he had heard from Bill that the inmates' favorite hymn was "Steal Away."

An entirely different view of the Unitarian minister came from the description of a fire in the parish hall of the Hills Congregational Church. It was discovered around 10:30 at night and fairly quickly extinguished after causing $12,000 worth of damage. Apparently the fire department at that time was largely volunteer and thus this mention in the *Wellesley Townsman*: "One of the best known of the amateur smoke eaters, Rev. William B. Rice, pastor of the Unitarian Church, received injuries to a foot during the fire."

Stories of Rice as prison chaplain and Rice as volunteer firefighter were two of the strongest memories shared by parishioners many years after his sudden death in 1970. It marked him as so different from any other individual labeled "pastor" that many people just loved him for it. Certainly it set him apart from any other minister of this congregation, possibly since Albert Buel Vorse.

Meanwhile down in the western part of Wellesley, the Universalists were establishing a foothold in what is known as the Fells area. The Universalist Church of America had organized a congregation that met in a farmhouse at 348 Weston Road, not far from its northern intersection with Route 9. They had appointed Rev. Dana Klotzle to be its first minister. Two years later the congregation flourished enough to have a functioning church school, a wide variety of social events, and a ten-child choir. They petitioned the Universalist Church of America for permission to erect a church, and within a year that petition was granted.

Apparently the Unitarian Church in Wellesley Hills was not quite reaching families in the large Fells area; eventually the Universalist church did reach many of them. They began to raise money for the new building but apparently did not raise as much as they wanted because the church that was built at 348 Weston Road was not as ambitious as the architect's sketch. In time the congregation's growth had reached its limit, and it began to decline to the point of being unable to afford a full-time minister. At this point—probably the late 1960s—some families transferred over to the Unitarian church. Others went elsewhere; however, all remained very proud of their Universalist identity.

In the annual minister's report of 1949, Bill Rice reflects on several years of amazing growth. He reports average attendance rising from 140 to 170 over several years. There were twenty-four baptisms in 1949, twenty-four new members, thirteen weddings, and fifteen funerals. He made 108 speeches or sermons. Rice concludes his report:

> Here in this town the promise of liberalism is bearing fruit. We are not a minority church but one recognized as a source of community leadership and strength. Our church school instead of being made up of a pitifully small group is the envy of the whole fellowship. Our various organizations are held to be musts for intelligent, socially conscious people. Above all our church is growing in reputation and achievement as a source of guidance and strength to those who honestly and fearlessly seek the highest in faith.

It was about this time that Bill Rice was beginning to realize the enormous burden of being the only professional to whom most of those hundreds of families would go for help with the normal and predictable problems of living and raising children. He found that "people expect a middle-aged cleric must have acquired enough experience to handle all problems. I hope I know just enough to know how little I know, and how little any other man not technically trained has any right to presume to meddle in people's privacies of mind and emotion."

Back then, many might have assumed that people they envied because they seemed to be better off are not prone to the normal difficulties of living in families. But these problems were often reflected in children going through the school system. Rice, along with several of his parishioners, enlisted the help of Dr. Erich Lindemann of the Harvard School of Public Health and Massachusetts General Health who was a pioneer in studies of grief and also an active Wellesley resident. Over three years they were able to get grants to demonstrate what we now know about the difficulties of living in wealthy suburbs such as Wellesley and also to find ways get help to people who are unable to afford counseling or who are too embarrassed and ashamed. By 1952, Human Relations Service, Inc. was formed, a counseling service then comprised mostly of counselors who worked part-time and often on a sliding scale. According to a *Boston Globe* article on HRS:

> Dr. Rice reports [the agency] has performed some remarkable things. "We have helped alcoholics, married couples ready to break up, boys and girls involved in tragic and trivial messes, people almost sick enough to become criminal, those discouraged enough to think of taking their own lives.
>
> "But beyond that the Service has been exploring 'the health in us,' because look how long the human race has held together and how happy many of us manage to be most of the time. . . .
>
> "Some psychiatrists are said to consider religion outmoded and even dangerous," said the officials of the service. "But we believe such a view quite mistaken. Religion is central to our health. Our staff want to learn from the churches and work with the clergy."

In 1951 church membership was at 750. Yearly membership numbers from this point forward were 754, 707, 767, 805, 799, 826, 849, 890, no number reported in 1959, and 895 in 1960. These numbers must be taken with a grain of salt; when a congregation suddenly gets this big it usually has no way of actually keeping track of who is coming and who is not. Suffice it to say they were a very large congregation with an activist minister.

Following are relatively small incidents in this decade but reflect what the Standing Committee had on its mind during that time.

The church was asked to outline its staffing procedures as a model to other large churches. Most of the staffing had been ad hoc, so trying to bring some order might have been a good thing.

Bill Rice was in charge of setting up summer worship services for his congregation, the Hills, and the Village churches. These services were conducted four Sundays in each of the churches with ministers selected by that congregation.

In September of 1954, they finally adopted the custom of having two people count the weekly collection as a protection against the possibility that anyone would be accused of pilfering the weekly collections.

Bill Rice pointed out that the committee system has two major problems. Some have not given any consideration to replacing their leadership so that when a committee head finally retires there is no one willing to take his/her place. Also, no one plans for any reality past next June.

The growth of the church increased the number of petty details to be resolved. Increasingly the board delegated Bill Rice with the authority to resolve what in past decades the board would have handled.

The property just east of the church, now called Rice House, came on the market for sale. It made no sense for anyone but the church to own it. They bought it and later leased it to Human Relations Service of Wellesley.

Bill Rice was overwhelmed with requests for weddings. Everyone knew church members got married at the church without cost to them, but many requests were coming from non-members and many wanted to negotiate the price. Bill was empowered to work out a contract for all church employees who needed to be compensated for non-member weddings and hold to it.

In 1956 the finance committee had compiled a "small" list of people who were in some way active in the church but had not made any financial pledge. They were empowered to send a letter to these folks asking what their intentions were.

Several times during this period the parish hall basement was flooded. In one instance, the town was deemed at fault for creating a parking lot off Maugus Avenue, but the board did not want to push the town to indemnify them. In other instances, some speculated that the drainage system around the church was at fault for not keeping the water away from the foundations. No real solution was found though many were speculated and some were tried.

In 1956, Bill Rice was asked to chair a commission to come up with a plan for merging the Unitarian and Universalist denominations. The Standing Committee agreed, somewhat reluctantly, expressing the hope that he would not become exhausted in the effort.

Within a few months the Standing Committee began to search for ways—mostly new buildings—to help them meet the challenge of their continuing growth.

CHAPTER 15

Building a New Church

CHURCH SCHOOL REGISTRATION in 1954 reached 340. In 1955 it rose to 381, and in 1956 the number was 416. The next year it was 429. The adult numbers rose as well, but anecdotal evidence suggests that many parents saw the church as important for their child's religious education but less so for their own. Whatever the real numbers, the church was crowded every Sunday. In December of 1956, a planning committee was appointed to study the options for relieving that crowding and to report back.

In 1957 the planning committee reported that it had hired an architect who had come up with two essentially different plans. The first plan was to build a wing of the church building that would be a new sanctuary. It might [or might not] include a basement underneath with staff offices and work areas. The rest of the church building, including the sanctuary, would be remodeled with the aim of creating as many classrooms as possible.

The second plan was to make the new wing of the church a religious education wing with the sanctuary expanded to include a larger seating capacity. This alternative would cost $40,000 less but would also necessitate closing the sanctuary for six months or more because of construction.

The Standing Committee unanimously recommended the first plan, which involved creating a new sanctuary and converting the older building into two floors of classrooms. Almost certainly the prospect of closing the church down for six months played a part in this vote. It is also possible that while earlier ministers of this congregation had an appreciation for what one minister called "our Medieval chapel," both ministers and parishioners felt quite differently in 1957 about the tone of their worship space and wanted something more modern.

A congregational meeting was called in September of 1957 to vote the go-ahead for this still vaguely described plan. At this point the congregation had apparently not seen any pictures or plans to give them a feel for what was being purposed. As the day of the meeting approached, they decided to put off a vote until December. As December approached they realized that whatever the outcome, there would still be a house on what was called the "Clapp property" just west of the church. Since this house might block the light coming into the new building, they voted to investigate the purchase of that house.

Also in December the congregation voted to proceed with fundraising although there was not as yet any agreement on what was being built. The vote was 109 in the affirmative and forty-eight in the negative. Bear in mind there were 849 members and more than 400 children at this time. It is doubtful that any professional fundraiser would have advised the church to go ahead with this little participation in the decision. Nonetheless they went ahead, confident perhaps that those they hoped would come through with large donations were on board.

In the early months of 1958, there was a question about whether or not to include a basement. Some thought that the basement could be built for staff offices and a staff work room, leaving other staff spaces to be rededicated to religious education. Bill Rice was advised to visit churches with such an arrangement, and he did. He returned with the clear opinion that he did not want this arrangement for the new Wellesley Hills church building.

At a special congregational meeting in May of 1958, the proposed project was presented. It consisted of building a new sanctuary and a complete explanation of the need for it. The members present unanimously affirmed the necessity for expanding to meet the needs of the future and voted 111 to twenty-one to go ahead.

In January the Standing Committee was asked to approve the purchase of an electric typewriter for staff use conducting the building campaign. The Standing Committee's opinion was that this would seem extravagant, considering the money they were asking from the congregation. So they voted to buy two manual typewriters instead. A month later it was reported that an anonymous donor, perhaps having seen Yankee frugality carried a bit too far, had given them an electric typewriter.

The advertising piece for the building campaign turned out to be a ten-page booklet. Its cover featured a picture of a mother and father in front of the Reverend William Rice. He is robed as he would be for a worship service and holding a beautiful baby while handing the baby a rose. The caption reads, "and more room for our children."

The headline on the first inside page is, "Not just a larger church but a finer one, and more room for our children." Inside the booklet are sketches of what the transformed church will look like. On the first floor of the old building are six classrooms. The "Memorial Study" or minister's study is converted into a chapel for the church school on Sunday as well as for small weddings or memorial services that arise. The new minister's study is moved to the second floor of Rice House. The ground floor, including the area under the parish hall, contains room for ten classrooms, storage, a nursery, and a quiet room where the Sharp Room now is located. The second floor of the old church contains seven classrooms.

An outside view shows the buildings as we now know them except that there is a walkway, partly covered and partly open, between the new sanctuary and the old church. Above the vestibule of the

Drawing of proposed, later modified new sanctuary

sanctuary is a very 1960s-style steeple that seems to contain a bell. The roof of the older church is plain—unadorned by any bell tower or by the cross that the founders deliberately placed across their steeple. There is no discussion of removing the cross, which would have been a sore point for some people. In any event the modernistic tower was eliminated from the new building, and the old steeple with its bell and cross was retained. Perhaps building a new tower and eliminating the older steeple were sacrificed to budgetary constraints, diplomacy, or a combination of the two.

The new sanctuary building was dedicated on January 24, 1960. Following is part of the Litany of Dedication that was used, with minor changes made for more comfortable reading. These words were probably penned by Bill Rice:

Minister: As we gather as members and friends of this church, we remember the men and women who in past generations gave of themselves and their resources that there might be a House for the worship of God, and for the strengthening of the bonds of [fellowship]; a visible symbol of a faith inspired by love and guided by knowledge.

Interior of new sanctuary, dedicated in 1960

Congregation: To the founders of this church and those who through the years have maintained and continued its heritage, we express our grateful remembrance.

Minister: Together we have wrought to build this House. We beheld the vision of a fair abode, and each gave according to their ability. The draughtsman with a pencil, the carpenter with a hammer, the painter with a brush have toiled to give substance to our dream. And now the work is done. With joyful hearts we enter into possession. Yet our possessing is not to ourselves alone, for on this festal day we dedicate this House to high and holy uses, to the worship of God in spirit and in truth, and to the service of [all] in righteousness and love.

Congregation: Here let no [one] be a stranger, nor any lack of friend, but let love of the brethren abound.

Dr. Phillip R Giles, general superintendent of the Universalist Church of America, gave the dedication prayer. Dr. John E. Wallace of the Hills Congregational Church gave the scripture reading. The Reverend Malcolm Sutherland, executive vice president of the American Unitarian Association, brought greetings. Dr. J. Rhyne Killian Jr., chairman of the Corporation of Massachusetts Institute of Technology, gave the address.

CHAPTER 16

Merger and Run
for UUA Presidency

SHORTLY BEFORE OR after plans for the new sanctuary had begun in 1956, Rev. Bill Rice was asked to become chairman of the Merger Commission that would seek ways to engineer understanding between the Unitarians and the Universalists and to find a path toward uniting the two denominations. Bill was a born and bred Universalist who was serving a highly successful Unitarian church, which gave him credibility in both camps and made him just the right nominee for this job.

The two denominations had talked with one another for a number of years. The Universalists, who were not gaining in numbers, had also flirted with Congregationalists and others. Yet the Unitarians were their closest cousins, which perhaps was part of the problem. While not expected to resolve the reservations of either side, Rice was asked to find a way for them to deal with what separated them. Many issues were involved.

First, each believed that the opposite side was more conservative or more liberal than the other. This is particularly true in relation to ideas of God or the Judeo Christian tradition. There were members in both denominations who would not abide anything that sounded like traditional Universalism, Unitarianism, Christianity, or theism. There were also members in each denomination who could not tolerate what they saw as the radical humanist, anti-God rhetoric in the other. Those who remained bitterly opposed to the merger remained so over this issue.

The sizes of the denominations differed greatly. The Unitarians had been growing rapidly in recent years. The Universalist growth was modest at best. For example, there was a Universalist church in Wellesley, but by this time it had reached its limits at around 100 members while the Unitarian Society was at 800 members and growing. It felt to the Universalists as if they were being swallowed up and their heritage diminished.

Each denomination was supported in part by endowments that were given by people, now deceased, specifically for Unitarian or Universalist works. There was a chance that a merger would make it possible for a small group of individuals or churches on either side to claim that they were the real heirs of the Unitarian or Universalist heritage and therefore entitled to the endowment monies.

Under the leadership of Samuel Atkins Eliot, Frederic May Eliot, and Dana McLean Greeley, the Unitarian denomination had become highly centralized in organization. It had developed a firm credentialing system for ministers and strong leadership in almost every department. The Universalist church, by contrast, had been decentralized from the beginning.

Another difference seems to have been the least mentioned in various discussions about the merger but was perhaps the "elephant in the living room." In the nineteenth century, the Reverend Thomas Starr King, a Unitarian but formerly Universalist minister, once quipped that the difference between Unitarians and Universalists was that the Universalists believed God was too good to damn humanity while the Unitarians believed humanity was too good to be damned. In other words, the Unitarians were upper class, well educated, and reasonably prosperous people for whom it was easy to believe in the goodness of upper-class humanity while the Universalists were working class folk who could more easily believe in a loving God.

I once served a Unitarian and a Universalist congregation in the same town. The Unitarians dressed in suits weekdays and took the train into Boston. The Universalists were firemen, policemen, postal carriers, social workers, and teachers, many of whom worked in the same community where they lived.

All these differences, particularly the perceived socio-economic difference, had made the coming together of the two denominations difficult for years. Yet the post-war years had placed the younger Unitarians and the younger Universalists on very similar paths. Wealth, upward mobility, and education had diminished the former differences for many. Simply put, the children of each denomination found it much easier to make common cause than their parents could have found.

The theological differences between the two groups had also eased largely because younger members of both groups had pulled away from the Judeo Christian God and more toward God as an abstract, philosophical idea with many leaning toward agnosticism or atheism.

The Merger Commission, headed by Bill Rice, was not tasked with promoting the consolidation of the two denominations. Rather, it was to provide a framework that would enable both groups to explore together their thoughts and feelings about merger and see where that led them. There were to be two votes in each denomination. The first was to be advisory—like a straw poll—and the second would be decisive. The first vote indicated that seventy-six percent of the Unitarians and seventy-four percent of the Universalists leaned favorably toward merger; seventy-five percent of both denominations favored continuing to talk about it.

Disagreements arose over the name of the new denomination. Former American Unitarian Association President Frederick May Eliot had proposed "The United Liberal Church of America" in hope of including Quakers and Ethical Culture. The vote in the Wellesley Hills congregation was typical of many: against any name without the word "Unitarian" in it and against any name with the word "liberal" in it. With this feedback from many congregations, the merger architects turned to something more like the present name: Unitarian Universalist.

The place of Christianity in Unitarian Universalism also caused considerable debate over whether to include in the statement of purpose a reference to "our" Judeo-Christian heritage or "the" Judeo-Christian heritage. The latter did not please everyone and profoundly displeased some, but it was a sop to those who would have preferred no reference to Christianity or God.

The consolidation of the American Unitarian Association and the Universalist Church of America happened in Boston in May of 1960. The final act took place in May of 1961. Now the new denomination needed to elect a leader. Unitarian Universalist Association historian Warren Ross wrote:

> The Universalists felt strongly that if the head of either denomination ran for the presidency it might result in a damaging us vs. them confrontation, and Phillip Giles [head of the Universalist Church], despite many pleas from his friends and supporters, refused to let his name be put forward. Dana Greeley, on the other hand, had no such compunctions. "I urged Dana to back out of it," Giles recalls, "because I thought neither of us should be president, that they ought to pick a third person, but he would never hear of it."

With Giles unwilling to run, the UCA board nominated William [Bill] Rice. Widely respected as a superb chairman of the Merger Commission, he is described by Ray Hopkins in the *Coles Oral History* as "a hard worker . . . who had a presence and a voice that boomed." That much he had in common with Dana Greeley, but in terms of policies he offered a clear choice. Unlike Greeley, Rice was committed to the weaker presidency envisioned by the Commission, while Greeley based his campaign on his vision of maintaining the growth momentum manifested by the UUA.

Politics is almost always a bruising game involving opposition that sometimes seems to be and is manufactured; friendships are often broken and not entirely repaired. The contest between Bill Rice and Dana Greeley was finally resolved in a vote that Greeley won by 1,135 to 980. It was a contest about shaping the life and character of a new denomination. Both sides threw themselves into it. Bill Rice and Dana Greeley had known each other since childhood in all of the ways that young religious liberals in the Boston area knew each other from their gatherings. Bill invested all of his energy and hope into this campaign, believing that his particular vision of the UUA should prevail. After he lost, some of his closest parishioners believed and told me, "He was never the same again."

CHAPTER 17

Summing Up a Distinguished Ministry

BILL RICE HAD a number of interns who were much loved by members of the congregation. Unfortunately, many do not appear in the records of the congregation nor do they linger in the memories of those who still remember those years, partly because an internship then was not what it is now. Today, an intern is expected to sample and learn all of the arts of ministry under the supervision of a senior minister who is expected to be trained for this supervisory role. Back in the fifties and sixties, an intern was a seminarian who was expected to develop some rapport with the junior- and senior-high groups, preach maybe one or at most two sermons, and grab whatever time the senior minister had to give.

Some interns, however, earned a special place in the hearts and minds of many members of the congregation. One of these was William R. Jones, an African American man from Kentucky who served the church in the late fifties. The fact that he came to Wellesley at all is a tribute to Bill Rice's genuinely liberal and anti-racist vision and the willingness of many members of the congregation to agree with him. What follows is from Bill Jones' final sermon in Wellesley, titled "A Backward Glance Then Farewell":

> Although the decision to become a Unitarian and a Unitarian minister has been fraught with painful consequences, if given the same situation again I feel my choice would still be the same. In spite of the often bitter and distasteful experiences associated with this choice, I would still count my last two-and-a-half years here as the most formative, influential, creative and happiest of my life. [He is referring to leaving the religion of his family and neighbors.] Throughout this crucial period you have unknowingly shaped and molded me. My indebtedness to you is immeasurable. You have been an inexhaustible source of courage as I hesitantly and anxiously navigated a course through the often choppy and often tempestuous sea of crucial choices. Your generous evaluation of my student ministry has been an encouraging and determining factor in my decision to enter the ministry. Your warm and generous acceptance of me has convinced me that a Negro in the Unitarian ministry, if not a reasonable probability, is at least not an impossibility. By your generosity and zealous concern for my welfare, you have made it distinctly easier for me to sell my decision to my family and fiancée. Dr. Rice could not have done more for his own son in helping me to secure a position for next year. As my mother said of your concern for my welfare, "I worry about your salvation, but I am relieved to know that at least you are among friends."
>
> I came to you frightened and very self-conscious of being a Negro. I recall all too vividly my first Sunday in this church. I sat approximately there. Though you did not seem hostile, I felt I was being watched and evaluated. I felt I was on trial. Now I leave you feeling for the first time completely human. The greatest appreciation I can give you as a Negro is to tell you that when in an all-white group no longer do I feel I am the fly in the buttermilk, but a Unitarian among fellow Unitarians, a friend among friends. . . .

> Last Sunday after announcing to the Junior Church that I would not be with them next year, one child came to me after the service and asked, "Do you have to go?" The sincere and honest regret in her eyes will always be one of my treasured memories. Still [another] image comes to mind as I glance backward. It is a picture taken from my first sermon to you. At that time I spoke of the concept of a magic circle, that inside of a magic or an imaginary magic circle you are protected, safe and favored. This magic of the magic circle most aptly describes my evaluation of my stay here at Wellesley. . . . I extend a full but insufficient appreciation for having been included in the circle of your neighborly love and concern.

William Ronald Jones was born in Louisville, Kentucky, earned a bachelor of arts degree from Howard University and a master of divinity from Harvard. Ordained by the Unitarian Society of Wellesley Hills, he earned a PhD in religious studies from Brown University. He served the Church of the Mediator in Providence, Rhode Island, from 1958 to 1960 and was a community minister and faculty member at Florida State University from 1977 to 2012, where he founded and directed the Department of African American Studies. Additionally, he served on the board of the UUA from 1993 to 2000. Bill Jones died on July 3, 2012.

When Jean Humphries married and resigned as director of religious education in 1961, the adult membership of the church was at 892, and 370 children were enrolled in the church school. The following year both figures went up to 929 and 400; however, over the next several years the adult membership dropped to 400. Starting in 1967 the number of children enrolled also began to decline steadily—probably reflecting children and their families who had not been coming for several years.

This same decline in church membership was going to happen throughout the denomination and throughout the country, but it would take some time before anyone would be able to spot that everyone was being hit with the same phenomenon. A demographic bubble had burst. In many communities the number of families wanting religious education for their children was declining. This is something that had not happened for at least two decades, and both lay and professional church leaders were not prepared for it. In addition there were parallel trends that rendered church involvement less important to young parents. To quote Bob Dylan, unofficial poet laureate of the age:

> *Come mothers and fathers*
> *Throughout the land*
> *And don't criticize*
> *What you can't understand*
> *Your sons and your daughters*
> *Are beyond your command*
> *Your old road is rapidly agin'*
> *Please get out of the new one if you can't lend a hand*
> *For the times they are a-changin'*

Whenever such a culture change comes upon us, many people in congregations react in ways they might later regret. This is happening right now in parts of the country where church school numbers are falling rapidly, leaving ministers and religious education directors to look toward each other for the cause. It also happened in the mid-to-late sixties.

In the church year 1965-66, Eileen Davis, the congregation's director of religious education, submitted her resignation. The Standing Committee accepted it. Then a minority of the committee argued that the whole matter should be reconsidered. Mrs. Davis asked to withdraw her resignation. The Standing Committee strongly but not unanimously reaffirmed their acceptance of her resignation.

Previously, Mrs. Davis had left the religious education office in Rice House and established her own office in the church building, which would suggest that a decisive prior break had occurred with Bill Rice and perhaps with the church staff. When she left the church a number of parents and children also left. Years later I met many of them when they returned for memorial services of old friends who also had stopped attending long ago. It was clear that their impression of the church as a moss-backed reactionary congregation had not changed, and their reaction to me was as mildly respectful as was possible. The 1965-66 church year was a sad time for everyone, including the minister and director of religious education. Though protagonists, after years of distinguished service they deserved better than having this unpleasant time hang over them.

At the same time, members of the Standing Committee were talking about calling an assistant minister. Bill Rice pointed out that comparable congregations had both a director of religious education and an assistant minister. This new minister would help him with his responsibilities, coordinate with religious education, and cover for him while he was on vacation so that he could have at least a month without any professional responsibilities. [This latter is simply astounding. Today and for many years, every minister is entitled to at least one month completely free of professional responsibilities. Not in 1966 Wellesley!] The Standing Committee voted that—at over 400 members—they could not afford another minister. They did call the Reverend Phillip Silk, a British Unitarian minister, to direct religious education.

In April of 1966, the Standing Committee was nonetheless concerned about the state of morale and opinion in the congregation, and so they commissioned a survey. Out of 550 surveys distributed, 137 "codable" responses were received or 25% of the total. The survey company considered this "a good return" and a "significant impression of interest and concern."

The results give an interesting portrait of the church at this time in its history: 80% were members of the Society; 60% were women and 40% were men. With respect to age, 25% were under 40, about

50% were 40-49, and 25% were older. Four out of five respondents were married; a typical response in any contemporary UU congregation would be quite different. Only 33% of the respondents were reared as Unitarians. Most others had come from a Protestant denomination, while 7% had been Catholics and 3% Jewish.

The survey concluded, "The Unitarian Society of Wellesley Hills is a dedicated organization, united in its fundamental loyalty to the goals of liberal religion. Despite some healthy and generally constructive criticism, the congregation by and large feels reasonably well served by its church program, supportive of its minister, and proud of its music. The measure of consensus on basic aims and issues overshadows discontent." Thus, the church made it through a tough time with the congregation fairly intact, reasonably satisfied, but perhaps with a lot of things left unsaid.

As time went on, the church governing board found itself involved once again in real estate issues. Since it was now known that Bill Rice would retire in 1970, some proposed selling the parsonage on Maugus Avenue and using the proceeds to pay off the debt created by building the new sanctuary. At the same time, others proposed buying the house just west of the church called the Clapp property. But what would they do with that house? Bill Rice and others argued that it would make a wonderful parsonage. Bill went so far as to argue that it would be a great place for the new minister to raise children, even though it was situated between the railroad tracks and the town's main street. Someone else suggested that the house be demolished and units for low-income housing be built. Another person suggested a home for elderly Unitarians be built on the lot.

Since the Rices were gradually transitioning to retirement in Francestown, New Hampshire, it was clear that they would have no further need of a parsonage. Checking with the UUA, the Standing Committee discovered that most ministers now preferred to own their own house rather than live in a parsonage and be granted a property allowance. Since there was little enthusiasm for launching in the direction of subsidized housing for the poor or elderly, the conclusion was to sell the parsonage for a good price, then to buy the Clapp property, and advertise it for resale for $1 for anyone who would move the house off the lot. That transaction was completed, and the house was carefully moved to a site off of Oakland Street where it is very handsomely situated.

Several other noteworthy events and issues arose toward the remainder of Bill Rice's tenure. First, I am often asked if the Unitarian Society merged with the Universalist church in the Fells area. The Unitarians made a very tentative offer at merger in 1964 and were turned down in such a way that the matter was considered closed. By this time some of the lay leaders of the Fells congregation had joined the Unitarian Society and became cherished members and friends. In recognition of that fact, it was later proposed to change the name of the Unitarian Society to the Unitarian Universalist Society of Wellesley Hills. The leadership then discovered that to make such a change fully legal, a large vote of the congregation and of the state legislature would be required. Therefore, they decided to let the matter of officially renaming the congregation wait for another day.

When the new sanctuary was built, the organ from the old sanctuary was transferred into the new choir loft, but it eventually proved to be prone to many of the ills of aging organs. The church purchased a new organ from the Andover Organ Company, and it was installed in 1972.

Finally it should be noted that during this period of buying and selling real estate and worrying about the minister's retirement, a group had been active on several issues concerning youth. In the minutes of a special meeting in 1970, the congregation approved a social concerns committee recommendation that $2,000 be divided among METCO, the Wellesley Youth Center, and the Wellesley Weston Hotline. METCO is a program through which selected children of color from Boston can enroll in the Wellesley school system. The Wellesley Weston Hotline, like many other hotlines in the area, was a way in which youth could seek help anonymously.

Bill Rice once told this story on himself. He was standing in the pulpit, white hair, flowing dark academic robe, deep stained-glass voice, about to launch into the prayer when he heard a young child whisper to his mother, "Mommy, is that God?" Apparently he used this occurrence to talk not about the God-like minister but about the lay leadership whom he had inspired and who made the Wellesley Hills church of the fifties and early sixties a model for the new denomination, which Bill also helped form and inspired.

Rev. William Brooks Rice

Rice was not the old-style great preacher whose charisma was based in part on his distance from the congregation. He was an effective administrator, an inspirational role model, and a thoughtful pastor and friend. He was a tireless worker for a congregation that was way too large for one minister to serve effectively. As the end of his ministry drew near, because he had announced the date of his retirement, the congregation voted him minister emeritus, only the second time they had conferred that distinction—the first being to Albert Buel Vorse.

In February of 1970, Bill went into the hospital for what was not considered serious surgery and suffered a fatal heart attack. In his memorial service, held on March 1, 1970, the service leader quoted the following reflection written by Bill Rice about an evening chapel service on Star Island in New Hampshire:

> Late one night I climbed a hill to the dark chapel near the top. The chapel is precious to so many of us—young and old. Good words have been spoken in it for generations. High hopes and noble dreams have had their beginnings in its fellowship of worship. That night young people came in, quietly, lighting it with their lanterns and their beautiful faces. A young man spoke words of poets, words of men and women of this age, troubled words, words which spoke of tragedy into which he must grow, under which he must grow in years. An ineffable sadness touched me, the silent spectator in the back, the one man of their parents' age and older. What was the portion of their inheritance they saw us giving them? What was the world which made them so sad in all their strength and beauty? They were holding the golden heresy of truth, a truth we had not wanted to behold. They were looking directly at a world divided by fear and anger. They were looking at it clearly and the wonder of it all was that there was no fear in the young man's voice, and no fear in their faces. We bred them. We lived before them in our homes. We worshipped with them in our churches. So much of their strength as they faced into the days to come was our strength. Their hearts were accepting the challenge of tragedy as if they meant to wrestle with it and drive it off. That earth might be fair and all men free.
>
> And quietly they walked out, leaving me in the silence. Down the hill they went—lovers holding hands, prepared to continue, strong to give their talents—and life too on the full honesty of holiness.

The following words were written on the occasion of Bill's receiving a degree of doctor of sacred theology from Starr King School of the Ministry:

- skilled in the arts of parish ministry
- pioneer in a community approach to human relations
- gifted in his ministry to students
- patriotic pacifist
- eloquent in the pulpit and unstinting in his service to the cause of liberal religion
- saved from the corrosive effects of ministerial success by personal integrity and a quick sense of humor

To the above was added, "known to us his parishioners since 1946 as our minister, our friend, our Bill, our Dr. Rice."

The following story comes from a sermon given by Judith Wells, a UU minister who had grown up in the church during Bill Rice's years:

> This church had a tradition . . . of inviting one of its college students to conduct the service on the Sunday between Christmas and New Year's. Dr. Rice invited me to do this in 1964 when I was a senior in college. I accepted immediately, then in November I had a personal experience that left me feeling unworthy so I wrote to him to back out of the service. When he received my letter, he phoned me immediately to find out what was wrong, and when I wouldn't tell him, he got in his car and drove out to Northampton in the worst rainstorm I can ever remember. He took me out to dinner and gently pried the story out of me, then assured me that what had happened did not make me unworthy to preach and he still wanted me to do it.
>
> So I came here that Sunday with my sermon about Mary and Martha, the sisters who were followers of Jesus and entertained him in their home. Mary sat at Jesus' feet and listened to him talk while Martha banged around in the kitchen complaining that she had to do all the work by herself, and Jesus admonished Martha that Mary had chosen the better part. As a young woman about to

graduate from college in the mid-sixties, who knew she was smart and capable—and who believed that women should be able to do anything that men could do—but who really just wanted to get married and keep house and have babies, I felt that I embodied the entire story of Mary and Martha in my own life. I still have the manuscript, with Bill's handwritten note at the top: "I appreciate this very much. It was good. WBR

After he conducted my wedding ceremony . . . before my husband and I turned to walk down the aisle, I stepped up and gave Bill a kiss on the cheek. I wanted that one kiss to tell him everything that was in my heart: I love you, thank you, you are so important to me, you will always be in my life. I hope he got it all because that was the last time I ever saw him, but he lives on in me and, I'm sure, in many of you as well, and I hope that his loving spirit still permeates this congregation as it once did.

A family of the church taught me a table grace that they learned from Bill Rice and used at all of their family's special occasions. The fact that nearly every member of the family, from young to old, could remember it reflects something of the legacy of this man:

O Lord, God, who hast called us thy servants to ventures of which we cannot see the ending, by paths as yet untrodden and through perils unknown, give us the faith to go out with good courage not knowing whether we go, but only that thy hand is leading us and thy love supporting us. Amen.

CHAPTER 18

Changing Course?

BILL RICE HAD announced his intention to resign long before he wrote out the actual resignation. He and his wife had moved from the parsonage to a rental house in Weston and were planning to retire to Francestown, New Hampshire. The news of Rice's retirement gave energy to very different groups of people.

One group wanted a very different style of church than what they had joined. Like most Protestant congregations, the Society was managed by an elected Standing Committee whose members had been carefully culled to run for office. Committee chairs also were well known to the Standing Committee, and they did a lot of the work. There was not a great deal of back and forth communication between the lay leadership and the large majority of members. Some of the younger members were talking about "lay involvement," by which they envisioned a widespread feeling of ownership among the members as opposed to "lay leadership" of a largely passive congregation.

A second and much larger group of people included many of those passive people. They had been happy enough to be members as long as their children were benefiting from the church school and they from listening to Bill Rice speak. They probably made a financial pledge but were pretty clear that they were there only as long as Bill was there and would probably leave when he did. The procession of members heading for the exits was about to begin.

In April of 1969, Phil Silk, the new minister of religious education, may have seen the way the congregation was headed but felt helpless to arrest it significantly. He wrote in his annual report to the congregation, "What we need most in this church is a rebirth of spirit. If people are excited about what the church can be, they will work together to create it. The gap between the ideal and the real has seemed to widen this year. I hope next year will see an increased enthusiasm, imagination, goodwill and involvement. Without vision and commitment, the church can do little."

The same annual meeting reflected that the church had 373 members, only 303 of whom were eligible to vote. Only a few years earlier the numbers had been up around 700 and 900; these new numbers reflected how insubstantial the church's growth may have been.

A long-range planning committee was appointed to give thought to some of the issues that needed to be considered in the search for a new minister. In October of 1969, the Standing Committee met with Theodore Webb, a representative of the UUA, who told them how to form a search committee and suggested that they probably could conduct a successful search in five to six months.

Now take a moment to think about that. When a beloved minister leaves—whether it is to retirement or because of death—the congregation needs to take some time to grieve. To suggest that they develop a stiff upper lip and soldier on to find a new minister in five or six months is similar to suggesting that we just "get over it" shortly after a close friend dies. Not only does it not work, but it has long-term consequences that affect both the next minister and the congregation—consequences that play out through the years to the detriment of everyone. Today the UUA recommends a two-year interim minister follow the departure of a beloved senior minister, because it takes at least a year for the congregation to stop hoping that someone like their beloved minister will come back and save them from their grief work. This view was not generally appreciated in 1969. Still very much minister-centered, the congregation wanted a new minister to be selected quickly.

In the past the Standing Committee had appointed a search committee based on what pleased them. This time they bent over backward to make sure that everyone was included who wanted to propose a name. Eventually a committee was appointed and encouraged to get to work as soon as possible. The long-range planning committee suggested:

> Because of our desire to involve everyone in planning our future, we recommend that appointment of a pulpit committee be deferred at this juncture. It may well be that the Society will decide that a pulpit committee should be appointed, but to appoint one at this time could create the feeling that the Standing Committee was moving to limit or prejudge the open review and planning we should like all of our adherents to take part in. . . .
>
> We do not think there is any urgency to have a successor to Dr. Rice standing in the wings a year from now. We believe the Society might even gain in some respects if it experiences a period with a minimum of professional leadership.

A search committee was formed and commissioned to go out to do their job as thoroughly but expediently as possible. Meanwhile it was January, and the finance committee was anticipating with some dread the next funds drive. On January 15, 1970, the finance committee made the first attempt at taking the case to the congregation. They wrote:

1970 will in more than one way be a year of testing for the Unitarian Society of Wellesley Hills. The search for a minister to succeed Dr. Rice is causing many of us to reexamine our ideas of what the functions of our church are and what they should be. The spirit of question and challenge abroad in the land is bound to be reflected in our thoughts, our discussions and eventually in our actions. Although the matter of ministry is near the heart of all this, it is by no means the only topic for consideration. Related subjects are far-ranging and it would be idle to assume that agreement on many of them will be unanimously achieved now or ever. . . .

The thing is, this Society is all of us. There are no "those guys." Your finance committee has good reason to know that no source and no one is going to carry us financially, and that commitment by all in the face of uncertainty is required. To that end it proposes to pull no punches, and you can expect to hear from us again.

On February 5 the same committee wrote:

The auguries are all bad. Church attendance is lower; church school attendance is far off; pledges were down last year from previous years. Fulfilling of pledges is down from previous years; the church surplus account will be empty at the end of this fiscal year. Yet we feel that your response to the new challenges facing the church will reaffirm your responsibilities to the church and the community; and we will, each of us, consider not whether we can increase our support to the church, but only whether we can afford not to increase our support to the church, thereby solidly basing the church's position as it goes forward into the changes ahead.

The perilous state of finances continued. Eventually it became clear that there would not be enough money to sustain the Reverend Phillip Silk's salary as minister of religious education. Though much appreciated by many people, he was caught in a situation that a minister with considerable charisma might have survived; but charisma was not one of his defining qualities. In his parting letter he wrote, "For the times we have helped each other I am grateful. For the times we have failed each other I am regretful. These have been important years in our lives and we shall always be part of each other. Here's to the future for all of us."

In a letter dated September 1, 1970, the pulpit committee announced its good news:

> We take pleasure in recommending to the parish that it call the Reverend Robert Erwin Senghas of Davis, California, to be its minister as soon as possible after January 1, 1971. Mr. Senghas, 42 years of age, is currently pastor of the Unitarian Church in Davis where he has served for the past seven years.
>
> A native of Cleveland, Ohio, Mr. Senghas graduated from Yale College in 1950 and from the Harvard Law School in 1953 with the degree of Doctor of Jurisprudence. From 1953 to 1955 he served on active duty with the U.S. Marine Corps first as an infantryman and then on legal duty as defense counsel and base legal assistance officer. After discharge he practiced law for five years with a prominent San Francisco law firm. In 1960 Mr. Senghas decided to change professions and embark on a career in the liberal church. He entered Starr King School for the Ministry and graduated in 1963 with the degree of Bachelor of Divinity. In addition to his duties as minster at Davis, Mr. Senghas is currently vice chairman of the Starr King Board of Trustees and was chairman of the faculty selection committee in 1968.

The letter went on to introduce his wife Dorothy Ann Senghas, known in Wellesley as Dorie, and their three children: Frederick age 17, Edward age 13, and Stuart age 5. It explains that Dorie was a Radcliffe graduate with a master of arts degree in history from the University at California. She had taught history at the University and in California secondary schools.

In his introductory sermon to the congregation, Senghas pointed out that the need for any church is less obvious than it was in times past. Many were asking why go to church at a time when belief in God no longer struck fear in the hearts of men and women if they believed in God at all. After a lengthy historical and sociological analysis of the nature and reasons for religion he concluded, "For me personally important as the church may be as an association of men and women whose principles I share, the <u>heart</u> [emphasis his] is in its community, the opportunity it gives us to confirm each other as human beings."

In his second sermon he quoted Emerson who complained that his own parish minister spoke at such a lofty level that one had not a hint that he had actually lived a life similar to the lives lived by his listeners. He pointed out that the life of a minister and congregation should be dynamic, consisting of challenges and responses on both sides. It was a life in which ministers and congregations grow together comforting each other when necessary but also afflicting one another with issues that must be faced. His concluding words may have puzzled some in the congregation as much as it pleased others. He said, "Yes, if I were called here I would afflict you, with what I pray would be a caring affliction. But affliction is not all that should occur, for if it is to be that we become bound together as minister and congregation then we should also celebrate together the gift of life, which we are granted, which is despite its transience, the glory of creation."

It would be fascinating to enter a time machine and encounter the world of October 1970. How would this new minister have been received? He was addressing the issues of the time: the source of religious authority, the questioning of church and religion, the doubts about God, and the importance of establishing a vital religious community rather than a passive congregation. Those who wanted the church to have a very different vision of its role should have been heartened.

Those who hoped for smart preaching should have been heartened, although Bob Senghas was clearly an intellectual in a way that Bill Rice was not. He was a young man, which they probably had been seeking. But he was short where Bill Rice was tall, and where Bill had a booming stained-glass voice, Bob did not. My guess is that those who may have been troubled by these differences were prepared to give the Reverend Senghas from California the benefit of a doubt and their great hopes for his success.

One of the outstanding issues of the day had to do with youth. The young people in Wellesley said they were bored; there was nothing for them to do. There was a perception that this boredom too easily led to experimentation with drugs, alienation from the values held by most adults, anger at the forced involvement of young people in a foreign war, and a vague interest in evangelical religious groups that were aggressively soliciting teens often without their parents' knowledge.

In response, many communities established hot lines—telephone numbers that would connect teens to adults who were "trained" to converse with troubled kids, helping them to avoid or get rid of addictive habits, suicidal thoughts, or to talk through problems with peers or parents to which most teens are prone. The social concerns committee of the Wellesley Unitarian Society established a hotline in the basement of the "old church." Somehow something like a drop-in center became associated with it.

The church became a magnet for youth from throughout the western suburbs who were seeking a place to connect with each other. In the process it also became a magnet for drug dealers. During this time, I was serving a church in Canton, Massachusetts, and volunteering on their hotline. I heard several times from callers that the Unitarian church in Wellesley was the place to get drugs. My co-workers heard the same thing.

On many Friday and Saturday nights the church lawn and parking lot were gathering places for local youth. The adults of the congregation who were there to engage with the kids were probably innocent of understanding the transactions that were going on all around them for what they were. But trespassing inside the church after hours, sleeping there overnight, break-ins, and vandalism were commonly discussed at Standing Committee meetings. Committees to deal with the issue were created and disbanded. Youth somehow discovered that if found in the church after hours they were to identify themselves as "LRY," the church youth group. Despite the fact that these weekend gatherings were taking place regularly over six or seven years, nowhere have I found in the minutes of any meeting that anyone said out loud, "Maybe we ought to close this thing down and make it clear that we do not want unaffiliated kids hanging around the church on Friday and Saturday nights." To do so was to be accused of being part of the problem.

The social concerns committee of the church had raised $3,000 for organizations that help young people. It had also raised $1,500 for Black Affairs Council bonds, a venture in black empowerment. Some saw this committee as a way of the church putting its money where its ideals implied it should go.

At the same time the church created an adult programs committee—something proposed by Bob Senghas and several members—to provide more variety and also lay leadership to several worship services each year. The church had been highly minister-centered since its founding, as had most Unitarian churches up until then. This new committee brought folk singers, older members of the congregation giving autobiographical reflections, sensitivity workshop leaders, and prominent speakers on a variety of topics. Because this format changed the usual order of service and sometimes eliminated hymns and choral anthems, there were objections; some folks stayed away. But overall the experiment was a foot in the door of greater flexibility in worship experiences.

In addition to being Bob Senghas' first full year as minister, 1971 was also the congregation's 100th anniversary. The Reverend Waitstill Sharp was the featured speaker at the celebration. In a meticulously researched and lengthy sermon, he led the congregation through its early days in which the Society was kept alive by the tireless effort and sacrifice of its small band of members. Marion Niles shared her own memories and those of church members she had known to flesh out the congregation's history and express her appreciation for where it had brought them. "We feel sure that the 67 signers and founders of this institution would be given pleasure and comfort and assurance that their work was not in vain could they look in upon this event," Niles said, "and would have confirmation of the belief that our treasurer expressed in her first anniversary report that *faith and works combined* will accomplish any proper work."

All was not well, however. With expanded activities owned by different constituencies in the church, there were also "turf wars." Marjory Brown, Standing Committee chair in the church year ending 1972, made these comments in her annual report: "All of these things have given a feeling of strength and confidence to the Church, but as I have worked more closely with the Church this year I have also been aware of underlying conflicts and dissatisfactions." She refers to the idea of "territorial imperatives" and then continues:

> In this church we are a group of about 300 people who hold in common a small territory. . . . It is inevitable that the many individuals and groups sharing this territory view it from the standpoint of their own responsibilities and interests. To the house and grounds chairman the territory may be viewed as something to be kept repaired. To the custodian it must be viewed as a place to be kept clean; to the Alliance over the summer it is a place to store rummage for the fall sale. To the minister and the organist the sanctuary and the organ loft are for worship and music and let there not be any idle smokers or coffee drinkers around. The LRY has its territory in the Youth Room so that when it roams the rest of the

plant the fur begins to fly. So too with hotliners—when they started invading from their lower basement we heard cries of "throw the rascals out." In addition to these problems from within the buildings we have been plagued by youthful trespassers who have beset us like a band of sorcerers' apprentices, leaving two more broken windows for every one repaired.

After commenting that one would think Unitarians ought to be able to sort this out, Marjorie noted that so far it seems still a work in progress. She thanked several people for their considerable commitment and help and then spoke of Bob Senghas. "But your minister was steadfast and calm. . . . He has the wisdom to stand by while the people of the church took initiative and responsibility for the management of their Society. As a result our church is stirring, stretching and growing. Thank you, Bob, for bringing to us through your wise and loving ministry the chance to discover our respective talents and to find that each of us can add his share to the strength of the whole."

Finances were a good-news, bad-news situation. In one year during this period the church raised $6,800 more than the previous year but came in $8,600 short of the amount needed. The congregation was growing again, and new members were pledging; but the rising cost of everything was depriving the congregation of anything like a feeling of victory. Despite this, a new organ was purchased from the Andover Organ Company, paid for by private donations.

In the 1972–73 annual report, church leaders reflected that it will take a while before the congregation can feel it will be secure from want. The increasing costs of everything were such that even if the congregation raised a bit more than last year—even if it were a good bit more—inflation would rob them of a sense of victory. Even though more than thirty new pledges came in, they were low and averaged about $79 each.

Many members of the congregation had been proud of being a pacesetting congregation in contributions to the UUA, but the cost of reaching that level again was far more than even the most optimistic could imagine raising. So the denominational budget item was cut considerably—a source of disappointment to many people.

Margaret Blattman, the congregation's new director of religious education, reported in 1972-73 that there were 120 children in the church school with the average attendance running between seventy and eighty. This was not at all bad for the times, but the congregation could remember that only six or seven years ago that number had been over 400 children. Now the congregation of adults numbered over 400. It had been twice that. Many lay leaders tend to associate increases or decreases in their figures with something either they or the minister have done well or poorly. Sometimes that is partly the case, but more often than not there is a constellation of demographic and economic factors that could not have been changed substantially.

At the Standing Committee meeting on October 11, 1973, Bob Senghas presented an issue that concerned him, along with suggestions for its eventual solution. "The issue is the adequacy and flexibility of the church environment to meet the needs of the congregation," he said. "Specifically, (1) the chapel is too inflexible; (2) the parish hall is dark, cold in effect, and has acoustic problems; and (3) the sanctuary, although good for formal services, is too formal for some services and also has acoustical defects." The Standing Committee voted to form a committee to "study the effect of the church environment in meeting the needs of the congregation."

As a result, Ed Lynn was asked to meet with the committee. Ed had been an architect who became a Unitarian Universalist minister with a particular interest in how a church's architecture affects or is reflected by what they do. Ed did meet with the committee, but no written indication of what he said can be found. Perhaps more immediate and pressing concerns focused the congregation's attention.

In March of 1974, the chairman of the finance committee wrote to the Standing Committee:

> In general our members have been responsive, though a large number (not the retired group) seem to be in a rut—30 pledging only what they pledged in the last two years; others reduced pledges or refused to pledge. Noting these facts, plus the decrease in the number of new pledges from 12 to 7, along with comments received via our pledge seeker team, our committee decided the time for a grassroots survey has arrived.
>
> We feel that our Society can remain healthy only by initiating a growth program. We must have more two-way communication. We must give our members more of what they desire in a church, and in so doing make them active in our church life. The resulting responsive program should draw in many new friends.
>
> In order to promptly start communications, we have prepared a questionnaire with specific easily answered questions that can be tabulated to form a base from which the Standing and Membership Committees can work. This mailing, as in the pledge campaign, would be followed up by phone to assure maximum response.

Congregational surveys often seem like the democratic thing to do, but there is often a hidden agenda. Many members who are perfectly satisfied with the church wonder why the survey is being taken, and they may or may not turn it in. Members who have a beef with the congregational leadership know that this survey is their chance to make their point, and under the cover of anonymity they make their response as negative as possible. In addition, the survey is often written so that negative responses count more than positive responses.

In late April of that year, members of the congregation received a letter from their minister saying in part, "Last night at our Annual

Meeting I announced that Robert West, President of the Unitarian Universalist Association, would this morning be presenting my name as his recommendation to fill the vacant position of Executive Vice President of the UUA. This morning the UUA Board of Trustees accepted his recommendation and did appoint me to this position. This means that I must resign as your minister."

Bob Senghas closed by saying, "I have a strong emotional bond

with you and I have a sense of great loss in leaving. I have grown to know many of you well, beneath the outward amenities. We have shared many joys and sorrows, and I will take these memories with me."

Rev. Robert E. Senghas, recent photo, now minister emeritus of First UU Society of Burlington, VT

Bob and his family stayed in Wellesley while he commuted into Boston to work at the UUA, and he was an absolute model of discretion, good judgment, and kindness to a colleague—in this instance to his successor—me. I could not have asked for more.

In a sermon preached a week or two after this letter went out, titled "On Our Church: Getting Down to Specifics," Bob shared his sense of how things were with the congregation. Much of his appraisal was very positive concerning the lay leaders with whom he had worked and fellow staff members. He said that when asked during the interview stage of his candidacy what he thought was the most pressing problem of the church, he wondered if there was enough of an overlap between two distinct groups of people in the church. He said, "A lot of you want to continue our program as it has been done. You want a traditional order of service, sermon centered, traditional music, and the advocacy of traditional religious liberal values."

Senghas added, "At the other end of the spectrum is a group which is much more concerned with personal change and growth. You who are in this group tend to be more interested in programs in which you can participate, programs which are less traditional services and more concerned with the opportunity to participate, more concerned with a process in which you can become personally involved."

He went on to suggest that the overlap between these groups now seems greater than he thought at the time he first made this observation. A variety of institutional concerns and personal proclivities of the minister might lean toward the more traditional group than toward the less traditional one. He urged the congregation to try harder to reach this balance between more traditional and less traditional without having to wait for its new minister to discover the need for it after three or four more years.

The search committee included this sermon in the packet they sent out to prospective candidates for this ministry.

CHAPTER 19

In the Interim

UPON HEARING OF the death or resignation of their minister, most congregations quickly assemble a pulpit committee to find a new minister. By the early 1970s, however, research and anecdotal evidence had established that those who immediately followed the long-term ministry of a beloved pastor were likely to have a very short tenure. It takes at least a year for a congregation to work through grieving the leader who just left and another year for them to accept the freedom they have been given to behave differently with their new minister.

Absent this year of grieving, a congregation's search committee is likely to choose someone who either reminds them of their former minister or someone who is the symbolic opposite of that minister. For instance, if the former minister was an introvert, the new minister will be an aggressive extrovert. Neither choice is likely to be successful for long, because it does not speak to all of the needs of the congregation. With this new knowledge weighing upon those who studied ministerial transitions, the vocation of interim ministry was born.

186 JOHN HAY NICHOLS

At first interim ministers were retired ministers looking to earn a few more years of income before they left ministry for good. Over time, however, interim ministers were younger men and women who were committed to the new calling of helping congregations in transition. Typically they spend one or two years in this effort with each congregation.

Those committed to interim ministry have several major goals:

- Help the congregation understand its history and what effect that history might have on the present.
- Evaluate how well the congregation is presently functioning.
- Extend that evaluation to staffing needs and how the leadership might function with a new minister.
- Strengthen the congregation's relationship with its denomination.
- Help the congregation to that point at which they are ready for new professional leadership and willing to say a proper goodbye to the interim minister.

Essential to all of this is that the interim minister commit to the proposition that he or she *cannot become* the settled minister of the congregation he or she serves as an interim minister. Almost every interim minister is told by members of the congregation more than once, "Many of us wish you could stay. Could you, please, please?" The answer, without hesitation, must be to the effect, "No I cannot. I signed a contract in which I agreed that I would not become your settled minister, and I intend to honor it." Usually this quiets the "draft the interim" movement. The reason for this policy is that if the interim minister allows himself/herself to be essentially running for the office of settled minister, then he/she is not doing the job of holding the congregation's feet to the fire so that they will realize what their needs and growth issues are.

During the months after Bob Senghas' resignation, the congregation first fielded a search committee. But probably because it appeared that the search process would take some time, they hired Rev. Polly Laughland, an interim minister who had served a neighboring church for two years.

Many in the congregation loved Laughland for a variety of reasons. She presented a distinctly feminine take on the ministry that they had never had before. She had a pastoral style both in preaching and in relationships. She seemed to reach out both to adults and children, both to men and women. She was ministering effectively to a congregation that had recently lost a beloved minister of twenty-five years and then lost their most recent minister after just four years. Unaware of all the issues involved, the congregation began to wonder why they could not just call the search off and appoint Laughland as their settled minister.

In her annual report to the congregation, Laughland wrote:

> The UUA policy that the interim minister cannot be considered for the permanent position has caused a number of you and me some frustration this year. I can understand the reasons for it but I am not thoroughly convinced that it does always serve the best interest of the churches and the denomination.
>
> However after carefully assessing where both church and denominational power lies, I feel that it would be very unwise to force its change by defying it—and I do not intend to do so.

What would have put a stop to any further agitation would have been a statement by the interim minister that "I have agreed to not become your settled minister for reasons that are good and sufficient and which I still support. Please do not carry this issue any further." What she said left the impression that she was being compelled by the

UUA to limit her tenure to two years and not become eligible to be the settled minister. Though she had misgivings about having to leave after her term was up, the impression was that she would do so for fear of the power of the UUA.

The UUA later established that it has no power or inclination to discipline ministers for breaking their contracts. The Unitarian Universalist Ministers Association has that power and would in this instance likely use it. This broader issue of denominational discipline continues to arise periodically.

The congregation held a special meeting on May 22, 1975, which began with the formation of ten small discussion groups. After an hour each group gave a majority and minority report on each of the following issues:

- UUA/UUMA policy. Some felt the policy should be upheld. Others felt it should be rescinded.
- There was unanimous agreement that the interim minister had done a fine job, with counseling and church school especially cited.
- Although they were asked if they would prefer a male minister, all agreed that the female interim minister had changed hearts and minds on that score.
- Other issues were mostly concern for Laughland and her future.
- The final question was, in essence, regardless of denominational policy, would you like to have the interim minister as our settled minister? The "consensus of the majority of groups" was affirmative.

Congregation members at this special meeting were then invited to vote on each of the following propositions:

- Call the interim minister as the settled minister of the congregation contingent upon her willingness to remain with the church. The vote was forth-nine yes, forty-five no.

- Continue the interim ministry and appeal to the UUA board for a modification or exception to be made to allow the interim minister to become the settled minister. The vote was thirty-nine yes, fifty-four no.

- Abide by the current policy and call a new minister. The vote was thirty yes, sixty-one no.

- Never again have an interim minister. The vote was twenty-eight yes, fifty-six no.

- Ask the search committee to include the interim minister as a candidate for the settled position. The vote was fifty-five yes, twenty-seven no.

- Were you for the interim minister when you came to this meeting? The vote was forty-nine yes, twenty-two no.

A motion passed to pass this information on to the Standing Committee. Motions failed to insist that the Standing Committee move to elect Laughland as the new settled minister.

Time passed. Summer came and went. No real resolution of the interim minister dilemma had been found. The search committee kept working. In fact they interviewed over forty-nine ministers for this position and finally settled on one minister they felt they could enthusiastically recommend. Rev. George "Kim" Beach was minister of the First Unitarian Church in Austin, Texas. He was a fine minister who went on to have a significant career, although he may have been a little closer to what had been the congregation's traditional profile than to what some of its "young turks" wanted for a radically experimental ministry.

In the same newsletter that announced Kim Beach's candidating week, Laughland wrote that they all had a great deal of grief with which to deal over the parting of interim minister and congregation that presumably the election of this candidate would bring to pass. Apparently a rumor went about during that week that a vote against the candidate would make it possible for the interim minister to accept the settled minister position. This was preposterous, but some believed it.

Candidating weeks are usually quite festive as congregants come to believe that the search committee made a good decision, but this one was a trial throughout, reflecting a seriously conflicted congregation. The final vote was eighty-one percent in favor of calling Kim Beach to be the next settled minister. Most ministers today will not accept a vote of less than ninety to ninety-five percent; a vote with nearly twenty percent opposition nearly guarantees a short, troubled ministry.

The candidate went home to think about what had happened and eventually sent a letter to the congregation in which he said, "I have searched my heart and mind over whether to accept your call to be minister. . . . I deeply appreciate the confidence that most of you placed in me by extending your call, but I have decided not to accept."

Beach pointed out that the Wellesley search committee had sought him out and convinced him to be a candidate and not otherwise. He always reserved the right to reject a call if he felt it not wise to accept. Beach continued:

> I felt a pang of disappointment . . . when the vote came out as it did—81% affirmative, counting abstentions in the total of 187 votes. This sense of disappointment arose primarily from the fact that in several meetings starting early in the candidating week, the confused and emotionally loaded issue of the tenure of the interim minister had come to the surface, and had been directly confronted; this openness seemed to be appreciated by all concerned and to hold

out the prospect for breaking through the apparent impasse. However, the vote and the underlying tone of various encounters during the week—the frequent implication for example, that my ministry would not sustain the kind of programs or common spirit generated by the Interim Minister—led me to conclude otherwise.

Since I had read, in the public announcement of my candidacy from the search committee, the original agreement between Laughland and the church that she should not be considered for the settled ministry, I assumed before coming . . . that this issue was in principle settled; that despite past disagreements or disappointments the congregation had made a decision around which to join ranks and move ahead. Many of you, I know, assumed the same thing; others did not. I was shocked when I read after arriving there, Laughland's statement in your newsletter—the same letter which announced my first candidating sermon. By speaking of the uncertainty of her future and of the "very real kind of grief" which she and the congregation alike would suffer, this statement seemed to say to the congregation that her ministry was being terminated without her consent. Or so it struck me, and I could well understand that under this circumstance those who wanted her ministry continued would find it difficult to accept a new minister.

Thus the termination of the interim ministry seemed to be happening by default, rather than group decision. As a result I would have entered your ministry with a significant, though hard to measure, residue of ambiguity whether a new minister was wanted. No doubt hearts and minds change, but the fact that the process had not taken place before—nor seemed to have progressed after—my arrival indicated the lack of a clear congregational decision.

Beach went on to defend the rules governing interim ministers and to suggest that possibly the rules were wrong or that his assessment of the situation was wrong, but he also said, "The very strong impression I got that week was that it was emotionally charged to an extent that many in the church had underestimated."

Beach suggested that he could have engaged—as some no doubt suggested to him—in a "rescue operation" to redeem the situation. But he had "the feeling during that week that my efforts in that regard would not be viewed as impartial."

Kim Beach suggested that the healthiest thing for the congregation to do would be to solve this issue on its own. And there it was left. They never really resolved the issue, and I was not given Kim Beach's letter of response to the congregation's call until I was called and in office as their next settled minister.

CHAPTER 20

A Brief Autobiography

I CANNOT WRITE this last chapter objectively because it is my story. I was the minister of this congregation from 1977 to 2000. I could call it autobiographical and go on at some length about the accomplishments of which I am proud, but I think the reader would be ill served by a lengthy song of myself. So I will make it a brief attempt to explain why I believe the congregation ended up in a pretty good place by the end of the century. But I need to start at the beginning.

While shaking hands in the reception line after my first candidating service, a member of the congregation gave me the first and last poison pen letter I have ever received. The writer wanted me to know that the only reason I had been asked to candidate in Wellesley Hills was my youth. The interim minister had been the minister everyone really wanted, and I was a sad second. I was further told that the church administrator and its music director would make all the decisions, and it would better for me to let them. In reality, both of these individuals could not have been more helpful over the years and did not make my decisions.

Through the week, as I picked up hints that there might be others in the congregation who were carrying a torch for the previous year's interim minister, I began to wonder if accepting this ministry would be a bad idea. I was having a fine ministry in Hinsdale, Illinois, and probably could mend some fences and continue on there for many years. I needed to find some perspective.

Bob Senghas was living in Wellesley. His wife and youngest child were active in the church. I wondered if he could be helpful. I called him, and he invited me over for dinner on Saturday night. Essentially he wanted to assure me that most members of this congregation would rally to the leadership of its new minister once they got to know him. In that hope, I accepted the call they extended to me the next day.

The first few years were difficult. In the previous five years there had been three search committees, and many in leadership positions had been on one of them or were married to someone who had participated. Those who had wanted Bob Senghas did not get to keep him for more than four years. Those who had wanted the interim minister did not get to keep her for more than two years. Some of those who searched for and found me did not get the hip, "with-it" young man they thought they called, because I turned out to be a bit more conservative.

Over those first five years, however, many new individuals and families began attending and—being innocent of what had gone before them—joined this church and supported its minister. Over the years to come, revisiting the disappointments of the past became less and less important to fewer and fewer people.

In the years that followed my arrival in Wellesley, average attendance increased from 109 to 164 people on Sunday. Under the steady and often creative leadership of Pat Ellenwood, church school registration increased from fifty when I started to 183 when I left. During this time our budget increased from $100,000 to $358,000.

When I arrived the church had no endowment funds. The congregation's leadership, being debt averse, had ploughed all bequests into the service of debt retirement. Eventually the word got around that if you do not want your bequests to be paying the church's bills, you need to either designate them for something specific or not make them at all. Thanks to a hard-working committee, an endowment was created and grew to $400,000 by the time I left in 2000.

In 1997 it became clear that the Society's facilities were badly in need of refurbishment, particularly in the realm of classrooms for our growing church school. The congregation raised $1,500,000 for this work. An adult meeting room named for Waitstill and Martha Sharp was also created, along with greatly expanded areas for parking and access for persons with disabilities.

Rev. John Hay Nichols

We created an adult learning community that offered a large selection of courses, and we developed a pastoral care committee that provided full visitation and emergency services for the entire congregation. We began a two-year program to become recognized by the UUA as a "Welcoming Congregation." This program concluded in May 2000 with a successful vote. We created from nothing an outreach budget of $20,000.

About two years before I left, the congregation's leadership and I along with that of several other local congregations confronted and defeated a right-wing attack on UUs and liberal Christians in the Wellesley area. Finally, over the years I supervised a number of intern ministers whose efforts enriched all of our lives. As I was leaving, the congregation created the John H. Nichols Scholarship Fund for Ministerial Interns in the amount of $100,000.

Since I left, the congregation has had two settled ministers and two interims in between. It is not for me to write their stories but simply to express my appreciation for their willingness to share the journey with people I have come to appreciate greatly.

Notes

When a citation is from the archives of the Unitarian Society of Wellesley Hills, the abbreviation "USWH" is used. Though some of these early files are stored in numbered record books, most are in unnumbered folders. Therefore, when no book or page number is given, it is because there is none. All photos are from USWH archives unless noted otherwise.

CHAPTER 1: WHO WAS JESUS?
1. **Transcendentalism is** . . . Mark W. Harris, *Historical Dictionary of Unitarian Universalism.* (Lanham, MD and Oxford: Scarecrow Press, 2004), 465.

CHAPTER 2: GATHERING A CONGREGATION
1. **They had a** . . . Louise Austin, unpublished memoir, USWH.
2. **There was a small** . . . Ibid.
3. **Maugus Hall—in** . . . Waitstill Sharp sermon, USWH.
4. **We hired the hall** . . . Austin memoir, USWH.
5. **One of our** . . . Ibid.
6. **Such a small** . . . Ibid.
7. **After our work** . . . Ibid.
8. **The Unitarian Society** . . . Ibid.
9. **The irresistible will** . . . Sharp sermon, USWH.
10. **No pew rentals** . . . Austin memoir, USWH.
11. **To change the name** . . . Standing Committee Minutes, USWH, April 1885.
12. **As the legislative** . . . Ibid., June 15, 1885.
13. **The life of** . . . Austin memoir, USWH.

CHAPTER 3: THEIR FIRST MINISTER

1. **How well he...** "Wellesley Hills Unitarian Society Mourns the Loss of the First Pastor," *Wellesley (MA) Townsman,* January 1899.
2. **Every time I** . . . Quoted in Austin memoir, USWH.
3. **He was quiet** . . . Gamaliel Bradford, *Early Days in Wellesley: Being Casual Recollections of Boyhood and Later Years, 1867-1881* (Wellesley, MA: Wellesley National Bank, 1929), 218.
4. **Rev. and Mrs.** . . . . Sharp sermon, "Three Score Years and Ten," USWH, March 7, 1941.
5. **Mrs. Vorse, called** . . . Ibid.
6. **On a certain** . . . Albert Vorse, *Our Town* (Wellesley, MA), November 1898.
7. **Ground between the** . . . Sharp sermon, "Three Score Years and Ten," USWH, March 7, 1941.
8. **A story is told** . . . This particular story is told in several places and may well be apocryphal.
9. **Edwards memorial service** . . . Austin memoir, USWH.
10. **His quiet influence** . . . *Our Town* (Wellesley, MA), February 1899.

CHAPTER 4: GETTING STARTED

1. **Resolved that in** . . . Annual Meeting records, USWH, 1879, 31.
2. **Although there was** . . . Ibid., 33.
3. **In 1880 after** . . . Ibid., 34.
4. **It was thought** . . . Special meeting of the congregation, USWH, March 8, 1886.
5. **Was a very forceful** . . . *Wellesley (MA) Courant,* December 6, 1888, 1.
6. **The new building** . . . Ibid.
7. **The building of** . . . Rebecca Eaton, Treasurer's Report, USWH Annual Reports, 1890.
8. **The Twentieth Anniversary** . . . Ibid., 1891.
9. **We meet tonight** . . . Mary Smith, USWH Standing Committee Minutes, 1891, 34.
10. **In a tender** . . . Ibid., 96.

CHAPTER 5: ONGOING CONCERNS
1. **In common with** . . . USWH Standing Committee Report, April 24, 1899, 210.
2. **The Unitarian church** . . . Robert C. Cotterell, *Roger Nash Baldwin and the American Civil Liberties Union* (NY: Columbia University Press, 2000).
3. **In the death** . . . USWH Annual Meeting Minutes, 1897, 196.
4. **His quiet dignity** . . . Standing Committee Report, USWH Annual Reports, 1899, 210.

CHAPTER 6: THEIR FIRST SERIOUS TEST
1. **A man of middle** . . . Wellesley (MA) *Our Town*, November 1899.
2. **An able and** . . . Ibid., December 1899.
3. **In the full vigor** . . . Ibid.
4. **Society really makes** . . . Ibid., December 1900.
5. **The Unitarian Club** . . . Ibid., January 1903.
6. **Came here from** . . . "Rev. John Snyder Talks of 'As Ye Sow,'" *Boston Daily Globe*, October 16, 1905.
7. **New Plays of** . . . Ibid., October 10, 1905.
8. **Resignation of Snyder** . . . USWH Standing Committee Minutes, November 12, 1908.
9. **His resignation was** . . . *Boston Daily Globe*, December 13, 1908.

CHAPTER 7: THE PERILS AND PROMISE OF GROWTH
1. **Wellesley had come** . . . Elizabeth M. Hinchcliffe, *Five Pounds Currency, Three Pounds Corn: Wellesley's Centennial Story* (Town of Wellesley, 1981), 65.
2. **Ramsey was born** . . . *Wellesley Townsman*, January 21, 1910.
3. **It has been gratifying** . . . USWH Annual Meeting, 1910, 74.
4. **The routine work** . . . USWH Minister's Report, 1912, 103.
5. **The pastoral duties** . . . Ibid., 1913, 119.
6. **He entered earnestly** . . . "Rev. William H. Ramsey," *Wellesley Townsman*, July 20, 1917.

7. **Mr. Ramsay was** . . . Marion Niles, unpublished manuscript, USWH.

CHAPTER 8: THROUGH WAR AND EPIDEMIC

1. **Well that can be** . . . Charles F. Potter, *The Preacher and I* (New York: Crown, 1951), 122.
2. **One of the many interesting** . . . Ibid., 125.
3. Photo of Potter is from the biography of Charles Frances Potter written by Richard Stringer-Hye in the *Dictionary of Unitarian and Universalist Biography*, an on-line resource of the Unitarian Universalist History & Heritage Society, http://uudb.org/articles/williamrice.html.
4. **Rang the bell** . . . Ibid., 127.
5. **Many of the church people** . . . Ibid., 127-8.
6. **Wellesley College had traditionally** . . . Ibid., 129.
7. **According to a review** . . . "First Sermon," *Wellesley Townsman*, April 12, 1918.
8. **The year just passed** . . . USWH Standing Committee Minutes, Annual Meeting, 1919, 200.
9. **In his report, Potter** . . . Ibid., 203.

CHAPTER 9: THE TWENTIES ARRIVE

1. **The decade of the twenties** . . . Sydney E. Ahlstrom, *A Religious History of the American People* (New Haven: Yale University Press, 1974), 895.
2. **And so began what looked** . . . Hinchcliffe, 77.
3. Photo of Swisher from *Wellesley Townsman*, June 9, 1933, 1.
4. **When church gatherings grow** . . . "Turkey Dinner at the Unitarian Parish House Overflows to the Maugus Club," *Wellesley Townsman*, November 12, 1920, 1.
5. **I have seen him walking by** . . . "Winton Spoke of the Fiftieth Anniversary of the Unitarian Society," *Wellesley Townsman*, November 20, 1921, 3.
6. **The life of the church** . . . Ibid., 7.
7. **We now have with us** . . . Ibid.
8. **Fine feathers make fine** . . . Text of advertisement that appeared in multiple issues of *Wellesley Townsman* in 1921.

9. **The church as presently organized...** "Rev. Mr. Swisher Talks to Free Religious Society," *Wellesley Townsman,* June 22, 1922, 4.
10. **100% growth in 4 years...** "Hills Unitarians Plan New Edifice," *Wellesley Townsman,* March 28, 1924, 1.
11. **A fire broke out...** "Serious Blaze at Unitarian Church," *Wellesley Townsman,* September 19, 1924, 1.
12. **Voiced for beauty...** "Gift of Mrs. L. V. Niles," *Wellesley Townsman,* December 12, 1924, 1.

CHAPTER 10: THE ECONOMIC BUBBLE BURSTS
1. **A strong desire on the part...** "All Churches Combine in Wellesley Society," *Boston Globe,* October 23, 1925.
2. **The new building is...** "New Parish House for Unitarian Church," *Wellesley Townsman,* March 2, 1929, 1.
3. **The outer circle consists...** "Rose Window," Ibid.
4. **The last ten years...** "Unitarians Surprise Mr. and Mrs. Swisher," *Wellesley Townsman,* May 9, 1930, 1.
5. **Preaching Mission sponsored by...** "Unitarian Preaching Mission," *Wellesley Townsman,* February 7, 1930.
6. **Then came the matter of Mrs. Dove...** USWH Standing Committee Minutes, December 22, 1930, 170-180.
7. **The Church of the Messiah...** "Resigns Local Pastorate," *Wellesley Townsman,* June 9, 1933.

CHAPTER 11: THE MINISTER AS SCHOLAR
1. **A renewed conviction...** James Luther Adams, "Taking Time Seriously" in *The Prophethood of All Believers,* ed. George K. Beach (Boston: Beacon Press, 1986), 36.
2. **Whereupon he [Crothers] said...** ———, *Not Without Dust and Heat: A Memoir* (Chicago: Exploration Press, 1995), 128.
3. **In an April 18, 1933, letter...** USWH Annual Meeting papers, April 25, 1933, exhibit A, 2.
4. **Over the years...** Adams, *Not Without Dust and Heat,* 151.
5. **During the year...** Standing Committee Report, USWH Annual Meeting, 1935.
6. **We believe this...** Ibid.
7. **Under our minister's...** Ibid.

8. Photo of Adams from Wikipedia, unknown source, and used with the blessing of the James Luther Adams Foundation.
9. **Neither today nor** ... Virgil E. Murdock, *The Institutional History of the American Unitarian Association* (Minns Lectureship Committee, 1976), 59.
10. **It is time for Unitarians** ... Ibid., 63.
11. **Unitarians agree** ... David Robinson, *The Unitarians and the Universalists* (Westport, CT: Greenwood Press, 1985), 163.
12. **It is with keen regret** ... James Luther Adams letter, USWH, September 8, 1935.

CHAPTER 12: THE MINISTER AS PROPHET
1. **Last August the unexpected** ... Luna Niles, Standing Committee Report, exhibit A, USWH Annual Meeting Minutes, 1936.
2. **The story of my** ... Report of the Minister, Ibid.
3. **Our church was most fortunate** ... Marion Niles, unpublished manuscript in USWH files.
4. **The story of my** ... Report of the Minister, USWH Annual Meeting Minutes, 1936.
5. Photo of Sharp from Sharp family archives and used with permission of Artemis Joukowsky, grandson of Waitstill and Martha Sharp.
6. **We feel that great good** ... "Ethics of Newspapers Discussed at Joint Meeting in Unitarian Parish Hall," *Wellesley Townsman*, February 4, 1938, 9.
7. **Those who heard** ... Ibid., 43.
8. **Under the present budget** ... David Hall, Music Committee Report, USWH Annual Reports, 1938.
9. **One is impressed** ... Marion Niles, Standing Committee Report, USWH Annual Reports, 1938.

CHAPTER 13: UNITARIAN MINISTER DECLARES WAR ON HITLER
1. Photo of Martha and Waitstill Sharp from Sharp family archives, used with permission of Artemis Joukowsky, grandson of Waitstill and Martha Sharp.

2. **The crisis in the church** . . . Marion Niles, Standing Committee Report, USWH Annual Reports, 1938.
3. **The chairman of the board** . . . Betty Baker, *Odyssey* (unpublished autobiography), written in 1985.
4. **Wellesley Pastor Urges** . . . "War Against the Nazis" *Boston Globe,* June 3, 1939.
5. **To say that the year** . . . Standing Committee Report, USWH Annual Reports, 1940.
6. **I have been impressed** . . . Ibid.
7. **In two years we have** . . . Minister's Report, USWH Annual Reports, 1941.
8. **I remember a sentence** . . . Ibid.
9. **After the events** . . . Ibid.
10. All Standing Committee issues are from various USWH records, 1939-41.
11. Artemis Joukowsky, *Defying the Nazis: The Sharps' War* (Boston: Beacon Press, 2016). Artemis, grandson of Waitstill and Martha Sharp, also codirected with Ken Burns the PBS documentary film *Defying the Nazis: The Sharps' War.*

CHAPTER 14: AN EXPLOSION OF NUMBERS
1. **Mr. Rice was the unanimous** . . . Letter to the parish written by the Standing Committee, June 19, 1945.
2. **The church has made** . . . Standing Committee report, USWH Annual Reports, 1947.
3. **In concluding, Killiam** . . . Ibid.
4. Photo of Rice is from the biography of William Rice written by Alan Seaburg in the *Dictionary of Unitarian and Universalist Biography,* an on-line resource of the Unitarian Universalist History & Heritage Society, http://uudb.org/articles/ william rice.html.
5. **In his annual minister's report** . . . Minister's Report, USWH Annual Reports, 1947.
6. **In the December 1948** . . . USWH Standing Committee Minutes, December 13, 1948.
7. **One of the best known** . . . "$12,000 Damage to Interior of Hills Congregational Parish House," *Wellesley Townsman,* December 30, 1948, 1.

8. **Here in this town** . . . Minister's Report, USWH Annual Reports, 1949.
9. **People expect a middle-aged cleric** . . . Ibid.
10. **Dr. Rice reports** . . . "An Upper Middle Class Suburb Tells How It's Getting Along," *Boston Globe,* April 17, 1952.

CHAPTER 15: BUILDING A NEW CHURCH

1. Photo of sanctuary interior appeared on the cover of the Order of Service for the Dedication Service, January 24, 1960.
2. **As we gather** . . . Order of Service, January 24, 1960. The author assumes the litany was written by Rev. William B. Rice.

CHAPTER 16: MERGER AND RUN FOR UUA PRESIDENCY

1. **The Universalists felt strongly** . . . Warren Ross, *The Premise and the Promise: The Story of the Unitarian Universalist Association* (Boston: Skinner House Books, 2001), 30.

CHAPTER 17: SUMMING UP A DISTINGUISHED MINISTRY

1. **Although the decision** . . . William R. Jones, *A Backward Glance Then Farewell,* USWH sermon archives.
2. **In April of 1966** . . . Survey, USWH Annual Reports, 1966.
3. Photo of Rice is from the biography of William Rice written by Alan Seaburg in the *Dictionary of Unitarian and Universalist Biography,* an on-line resource of the Unitarian Universalist History & Heritage Society, http://uudb.org/articles/ william rice.html.
4. **Late one night** . . . "Reflection on a Star Island Chapel Service," in "Memorial Service for William Brooks Rice," USWH papers, 1970.
5. **The church had a tradition** . . . Judith Wells, "A Child of the Church Comes Home," author's papers.

CHAPTER 18: CHANGING COURSE?

1. **Because of our desire** . . . Long-Range Committee Report, USWH, 1969.

2. **1970 will in more**... Finance Committee Letter #1, USWH, January 15, 1970.
3. **The auguries are**... Finance Committee Letter #3, USWH, February 5, 1970.
4. **In his parting letter** . . . Phil Silk, Letter of Resignation, USWH, April 13, 1970.
5. **We take pleasure** . . . Ministerial Search Committee announcement, USWH, September 1, 1970.
6. **For me personally** . . . Robert Senghas sermon, "New Reasons for an Old Church," USWH, October 1970.
7. **Yes, if I were called** . . . ———, "The Affliction Called the Ministry," USWH, October 1970.
8. **We feel sure** . . . Marion Niles, unpublished manuscript, USWH, 1971.
9. **All of these things** . . . Marjorie Brown, Standing Committee Report, USWH Annual Reports, 1972.
10. **But your minister**... Ibid.
11. **The issue is** . . . USWH Standing Committee Minutes, October 11, 1973.
12. **In general our members**... Finance Committee Memo, USWH, October 11, 1973.
13. **Last night at** . . . Robert Senghas, Letter to the Congregation, USWH, April 26, 1974.
14. Photo of Senghas used with permission of photographer, Gillian Randall of Gillian Randall Photography, Charlotte, VT, who profiled Bob Senghas on her photography blog at vtsenior.blogspot.com/search?q=senghas.
15. **A lot of you**... Robert Senghas, "On Our Church Getting on to Specifics," USWH Sermons, May 19, 1974.

CHAPTER 19: IN THE INTERIM

1. **The UUA policy**... Polly Laughland, Report of the Interim Minister, USWH Annual Meeting Minutes, 1975.
2. **UUA/UU Ministers Association policy** . . . Minutes of Special Meeting of the Congregation, USWH, May 22, 1975.
3. **I have searched**... Kim Beach, Letter to the Congregation, USWH, April 26, 1974.

CHAPTER 20: A BRIEF AUTOBIOGRAPHY

1. Photo of Nichols by Damianos Photography is from John Nichols' personal collection.

ABOUT THE AUTHOR

The Reverend Dr. John Hay Nichols is minister emeritus of the Unitarian Universalist Society of Wellesley Hills, Massachusetts, where he served as senior minister for twenty-three years. Previously, he was minister in Hinsdale, Illinois, and Canton, Massachusetts. Before retiring, John served as interim minister for ten congregations in Massachusetts, Rhode Island, and New York.

Nichols received his Doctor of Ministry degree from Meadville Theological School in Chicago and has taught Unitarian Universalist Polity at Andover Newton Theological School and New York Theological Seminary. He is the author of *A Wind Swept Over the Waters: Reflections on Sixty Favorite Bible Passages*, *A Biblical Humanist Companion*, *Liberal Religion's Response to Loss*, and numerous other publications.

John and his wife Nancy live in Wayland, Massachusetts, and enjoy spending time with their two children and five grandchildren.

66958932R00125

Made in the USA
Charleston, SC
31 January 2017